Kids can Knit

Kids can Knit

Fun and easy projects for your small knitter

Carolyn Clewer

BARRON'S

All inquiries should be addressed to:
Barron's Educational Series, Inc.
250 Wireless Boulevard
Hauppauge, NY 11788
http://www.barronseduc.com

Library of Congress Catalog Card Number: 2002116525

ISBN - 13: 978 0-7641-2718-2

ISBN - 10: 0-7641-2718-7

Conceived, designed, and produced by
Quarto Publishing plc
The Old Brewery
6 Blundell Street
London N7 9BH

QUAR: KFK

Project editor: Michelle Pickering
Art editor: Anna Knight
Assistant art director: Penny Cobb
Copy editor: Claire Waite-Brown
Pattern checker: Pauline Hornsby
Designer: Caroline Grimshaw
Illustrator: Coral Mula
Photographer: Paul Forrester
Indexer: Madaleine Combie

Art director: Moira Clinch
Publisher: Piers Spence

Manufactured by Universal Graphics Pte Ltd, Singapore
Printed by Star Standard Industries (Pte) Ltd, Singapore

9 8 7 6 5 4 3 2

Contents

2/8/06

Introduction

Knitting is a way of making a stretchy fabric from a long length of yarn. For hundreds of years, all sorts of people have knitted all kinds of things, all over the world. You can knit crazy and original things as well as useful and practical ones. Once you have started to knit, you will discover a fun and creative hobby to continue for the rest of your life.

Hand knitting

When you look at a sweater or a woolly scarf, you can clearly see if it has been knitted. The knitting in this book is hand knitting, which is simple to learn and fun to do. Sometimes things are knitted by machine, which is faster. The stitches can be much finer, but they are still made in the same way. Some T-shirts, socks, and even dishcloths are machine knitted. The projects in this book teach you how to hand knit. You will find out how to use the basic equipment and materials, and by following step-by-step instructions and colorful illustrations, you will master simple techniques to make 16 lively projects.

Learning step by step

Every time a new skill is introduced, there is a project that you can follow to practice it. Starting with finger knitting, you can have fun using colorful yarns, and you will soon discover how easy it is to cast on and knit with needles. You will learn simple knitting techniques while making exciting items for yourself and for friends. You will enjoy picking up new skills, like shaping, while knitting fried eggs, and trying out purl stitch on a string of silly sausages. Following these projects are instructions for making garments that you can wear, like a poncho, a Peruvian hat, and a striped sweater. If you run out of yarn and want to keep knitting, there's even a chapter that offers ideas for how to make your own "yarn."

Fun with friends

You can knit on your own or with other people. You can learn about knitting in private by following the projects and instructions in this book, but it's also fun to ask for extra help and ideas from friends and family who can already knit. Just like drawing, cooking, or telling stories, everyone has his or her own way of knitting, so if somebody shows you a different way of doing things, try it and see which method you prefer. Maybe a friend would like to learn with you. Perhaps you will even be asked to help other friends to learn once you have worked through the book.

What next?

Working through this book will give you lots of practice and confidence in all knitting skills. You can then try working from other knitting patterns or enjoy inventing some ideas and color combinations of your own. So after you have made these projects, all you need to do is decide what to knit next!

Materials

Yarn is the most important material you will need when knitting. Any yarn can be used to knit. Later in the book, you will even learn how to make your own yarn. Of course, the more you like the texture and color of a yarn, the more fun knitting with it will be. You will find it easier to learn to knit with yarn that is simple to use, so try using smooth worsted yarn or thick bulky yarn when practicing.

Yarn

Whether you shop in your local yarn or craft store, you will realize that yarn comes in all different colors, thicknesses, and textures. Leftover yarn pieces are useful to practice with or to use for embroidering and trimming projects, so save those odd bits in a bag.

Weight

Most projects and patterns suggest the weight or thickness of yarn that should be used to get good results. These are some of the most common weights available:

 Extra-bulky yarn is a really fat yarn that you knit on giant needles.

Bulky yarn is a thick yarn often used for knitting warm winter sweaters.

Aran or fisherman yarn is a medium-weight yarn that is a good weight for beginners to start with.

Worsted yarn is a popular weight for all sorts of projects. It is slightly thinner than Aran and is also easy to use.

 Sport yarn is a finer weight than worsted and is knitted on thin needles.

Fingering yarn is very fine.

 Fancy yarns like metallic, shiny, chenille, and tape yarns come in all sorts of thicknesses and can give interesting effects to your knitting.

Fluffy yarns like mohair are usually knitted more loosely. Kid mohair is finer and can be knitted like sport or worsted yarn. Luxury or bulky mohair can be knitted like Aran or bulky yarn.

Fibers

Most yarn is made by spinning or twisting fibers together. Both natural and synthetic fibers can be used to make yarn.

Wool is a natural fiber that is spun from sheep's fleece. It is good to knit with and warm to wear.

Mohair is a yarn that is made from goat hair. The long hairs are very fuzzy and fluffy.

Cotton is made from plants. It is cool to wear and easy to wash.

Acrylic, polyester, nylon, and other synthetic fibers are man-made and often mixed with natural fibers.

Ball band information

Most yarn comes in balls or hanks, which are labeled with a lot of information on the band. Look closely at a ball band to find out everything you need to know about the yarn.

● Manufacturer's name and yarn type—This tells you what the yarn is called and who made it.
● Weight and length—This will help you figure out how many balls of yarn you need to knit your project or pattern.
● Fiber content—This tells you what the yarn is made of.
● Shade—This is the yarn maker's name or number for the yarn color.
● Dye lot—This is a number that shows which balls of yarn were dyed at the same time. If you are using more than one ball of yarn in the same shade, make sure that they have the same dye lot number so that they are an exact match.
● Needle size—This is the recommended needle size for the yarn. It is a good guide, but if your knitting is a bit tight you may need to use a bigger needle size, or if your knitting is a bit loose, you may need to use a smaller needle size. We'll explain more about this on page 92.
● Gauge—The gauge helps you figure out the number of stitches and rows you need to get your knitting the right size. Stitches knitted in thin yarn are smaller than stitches knitted in thick yarn. Gauge is explained in more detail on page 92.
● Washing instructions—This information is usually shown as symbols that explain how you should wash and care for your knitting to keep it at its best (see page 125).

Trims

Trims are the buttons, sequins, beads, ribbons, and braids that are used to finish and decorate the things you knit. Look around a sewing or craft store to see what is available. You can also start collecting buttons from worn-out clothes and beads from broken necklaces. Use a jar or container with a lid to store pretty or colorful trims as you find them. You will soon have a treasure trove.

Other materials

Some projects require special materials that should be available from most craft stores. Or, you can substitute store-bought items with household ones. For example, a pair of matching buttons can replace toy eyes; safety pins can become clips for pins; cut-up clean pantyhose or absorbent cotton can be used instead of toy stuffing. Keep your mind open and start collecting.

Kids Yarn Co.

Hand-knit worsted cotton

1¾oz (50g)

Approx. length 95yds (85m)

100% cotton
Shade 43 Lot A12

40°C 104°F Machine wash
Warm iron
Do not bleach
Dry cleanable in all solvents
Do not tumble dry Dry flat out of direct sunlight

20sts
4in (10cm)
4in (10cm)
28 rows
Size 6
4mm

This is an example of a ball band. Keep it safe because it contains lots of important information about the yarn.

Equipment

When you start knitting, you will need to get some special equipment that you can buy from a craft or yarn store, or perhaps a thrift shop. Or, you may be able to borrow this equipment from another knitter. At first you will need just knitting needles and scissors in order to practice the knit stitch. All projects in this book list the equipment needed so you can be sure that you have everything before you start.

As you knit more often, you will soon build up a collection of useful things, so it is a good idea to use a tote bag to keep everything safe and clean. Don't use an unlined knitted bag because the needles will keep slipping through the holes.

Knitting needles

Knitting needles are good value for the money because they will last for years if you take care of them. If the points become damaged or the needles bent, it's time to throw them out and buy new ones.

● Straight single-pointed needles come in pairs and are available in lots of different sizes. They can be fat or thin to suit different yarns, and short or long to fit the number of stitches easily. Needles come in different sizes that tell you how fat or thin they are. For example, size 19 (15mm) are really fat needles and size 0 (2mm) are really thin. The size is usually written on the knob at one end of the needle. Choose a pair of straight needles between sizes 6 and 10 (4mm and 6mm) when you are learning to knit. Needles can be made of plastic, wood, or metal.

● Double-pointed needles are used for "knitting in the round" (you'll learn about this on pages 98–101). They are usually sold in sets of four or five.

● Circular needles are also used for knitting in the round. The two pointed needles are joined by a flexible cord. You can also use them like straight needles to knit flat pieces.

Spool knitter

This is used instead of needles to make a narrow tube of knitting. Spool knitters are not usually designed to work with very thick yarns, but they can be used with different kinds of medium-weight and finer yarns.

Scissors

You will need a sharp pair of scissors to cut through the yarn easily.

Tape measure

You will need this to measure your knitting to make sure it is the right size.

Tapestry or yarn needle

This is a sewing or darning needle with a blunt tip and a large hole. It is used to sew pieces of knitting together and to weave in loose ends of yarn.

Stitch holder

A stitch holder is sometimes used on shaped knitting to hold some stitches safely while they are not being knitted. There are different types of stitch holders available to do the same job. You can even use a smooth yarn or string, such as cotton, to hold stitches. If you don't have a stitch holder, you can use an empty needle with a ball of putty or modeling clay stuck on the pointed end to stop the stitches from falling off, or a large safety pin to hold a few stitches.

Crochet hook

A crochet hook is used for making fringe or picking up dropped stitches. Crochet hooks come in different sizes. A size G or H (4–5mm) hook is useful to have.

Pins

These are used for holding the knitting in position before sewing pieces together. Large-headed pins are good to use because they don't fall through the knitting.

Point protectors

These can be used to stop stitches from falling off the needles when you put your knitting down or carry it around.

Stitch markers

These are small plastic or metal rings that you can slip into your knitting or onto a needle to mark a particular stitch or row. If you don't have any, you can simply use a safety pin or make a marker from a piece of contrasting colored yarn instead (see page 99).

Row counter

It's important to count the number of rows when you are making some projects. You can fit a row counter close to the knob of a straight needle and turn the dial every time you finish a row. Don't worry if you don't have one—you can just as easily keep count with a pencil and paper instead.

Playing with yarn

Before you start to knit, it's a good idea to experiment with a few different types of yarn to see how they look and feel. The easiest and most enjoyable way to do this is by learning some basic knitting skills that don't require needles. The simplest sort of knitting is finger knitting. It is really easy to do and you can use any yarn you can find. It will also help you to learn how a knitted stitch is formed out of a loop of yarn. In this chapter you will also find out how to make a tube of knitting using a spool knitter, and how to make fluffy pompoms and braids.

Finger knitting

Finger knitting is an easy way of knitting a chain of yarn without using knitting needles. Worsted-weight or bulky yarn is easy to use when learning new techniques, but you can try finger knitting with any yarn.

When we refer to the "working end" of the yarn, this simply means the end that comes from the ball. The loose end is therefore the other end.

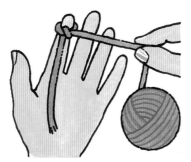

1 Tie the loose end of the yarn around your index finger. Hold your hand with your palm facing you. Keep the loose end of the yarn against your palm and hold the working end in your other hand.

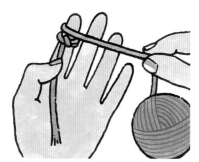

2 Wrap the working end of the yarn once around your index finger, ending just above the knot. You now have two loops around your finger.

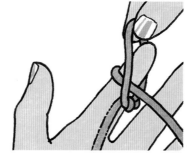

3 Let go of the working end and use your fingers to lift the bottom loop up over the top loop.

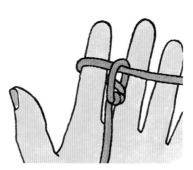

4 Drop this loop off the end of your finger, leaving just one loop on your finger once again.

5 Now wrap the working end of the yarn around your finger above the loop. Lift the bottom loop over the top loop and drop it, just like you did before in Steps 3–4.

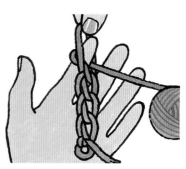

6 Follow Steps 3–5 to continue making the chain in the same way. You can make the chain as long as you want, or just keep practicing until you get the hang of it.

7 To finish, cut the working end of the yarn about 4 inches (10cm) from the end of the chain. Gently slide your finger out of the last loop. Thread the cut end of the yarn through the loop and pull tightly to seal the chain.

Spool knitting

Spool knitting, also known as French knitting, is a way of making knitted tubular cords that can be used as drawstrings, ties, decoration, or even shoelaces. You will need a spool knitter, some sport- or worsted-weight yarn, a knitting needle, and a tapestry needle.

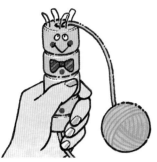

1 Push the loose end of the yarn down the center hole of the spool and grip this end with the same hand that is holding the spool.

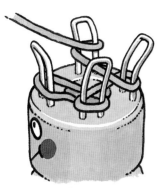

2 Use your other hand to loop the working end of the yarn around each of the pegs one by one. Make sure that you loop the yarn around all the pegs in the same direction, either clockwise or counterclockwise.

3 When you have looped the yarn back around to the beginning, pass it in front of the first peg. Then use a knitting needle to lift the bottom loop over the working end of the yarn.

4 Use the knitting needle to lift the loop right off the peg and drop it into the center hole. You now have a new loop on the peg.

5 Pass the working end of the yarn in front of the next peg and repeat Steps 3–4, remembering to grip the tail end of the yarn tightly and to work in the same direction around the pegs.

6 When the tube of knitting is as long as you wish, lift the last stitch that you knitted right off the peg and put it onto the next peg. You now have two stitches on the second peg. Lift the bottom stitch up and over the top stitch. Continue moving each stitch across to the next peg until you have only one stitch left.

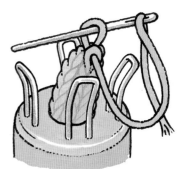

7 Cut the yarn about 6 inches (15cm) from the knitting. Gently lift the last stitch up from the peg. Use a tapestry needle to thread the end of the yarn through the last stitch and pull tightly to fasten. Pull the knitting out of the spool.

Making pompoms

Pompoms can be made from all sorts of yarn, but for the best results use woolly or fluffy ones. You could even combine different colors and weights of yarn. About 30–40 yards (30–40m) of worsted-weight or bulky yarn will make a 4-inch (10cm) pompom. You will also need some cardboard, such as an empty cereal box, and two small dishes or jars to draw around to make the circles.

1 Draw two circles of about 4 inches (10cm) in diameter onto a piece of cardboard. Cut them out. Draw a 2-inch (5cm) diameter circle in the center of both disks. Cut a slit into the disks from the outside edge and cut out the center circles.

3 Put the two disks together and make sure that the slits you cut in Step 1 are not in the same place.

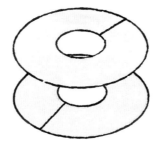

5 Insert one blade of a pair of scissors between the two disks and cut into the yarn. Work around the edge until all the yarn is cut.

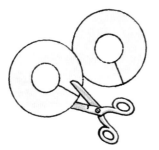

2 Wind some small balls of yarn that will fit through the hole. To do this, wrap the yarn loosely a few times around your fingers. Then take it off your fingers and wrap some more yarn around the first wraps, stopping before it gets too big.

4 Hold the disks together and wind some yarn around and around the disks to cover them. When one ball of yarn runs out, simply start another. Continue until the center hole is too small to get any yarn through.

6 Pull the disks apart slightly and tie a length of strong yarn tightly around the middle of the pompom between the disks. Wrap the yarn around again and tie a double knot to make sure it is really secure. Leave the ties long enough to use when sewing or tying the pompom into place. Remove the two disks and fluff out your pompom.

Braiding

Braiding yarn is just like braiding hair and it's a really useful way of making a trim or tie for your knitting. To practice braiding, use a thick yarn that is easy to work with. Once you have mastered the technique, try braiding together three equal-sized bunches of different colored yarns to make a decorative pattern.

1 Cut three strands of yarn to the same length. About 8 inches (20cm) would be good to start. Knot the strands together at one end.

2 Use masking tape to fix the knotted end to a secure surface, such as a clipboard, or ask a friend to hold it for you. Whatever you do, don't stick it to your mom's favorite table.

3 Separate the three strands so that you can clearly see one in the middle and one on either side. Pick up the right-hand strand and place it over the middle strand.

4 Now pick up the left-hand strand and place it over the new middle strand.

5 Pick up the new right-hand strand and put it over the new middle strand.

6 Continue like this, putting the left and then the right strands over the middle one.

7 When your braid is long enough, or you run out of yarn, tie all the strands in a knot at the bottom end to stop it from coming undone. Alternately, tie another strand of yarn, an elastic band, or a ribbon around the loose ends.

Spooky spider toy

Now that you know how to finger knit, spool knit, and make pompoms, let's put all these skills together to make a scary, hairy, pompom spider with a big furry body and long, long legs. You can mix up any types of yarn, but thick fluffy wool is best for a really big and furry spider. Decide whether you want spidery black or if you would prefer to use up remnants of yarn for a multicolored creation. Whatever you choose, you'll have fun making your new toy.

You are now going to use the skills you learned on pages 14–16. If you need a reminder of how to do something, just refer to the pictures and instructions there.

Making the string

▲ Make a length of finger knitting to dangle the spider.

1 Make a really long length of finger knitting. It should be at least 3 feet (1m) long to give you lots of dangling fun.

Knitting the legs

▲ Make four lengths of spool knitting for the spider's legs.

1 Make four 1-foot (30cm) lengths of spool knitting. Remember to fasten off all the strips so that they don't unravel. These strips will become eight long spider legs. You could make them all the same color, all different, or try alternate colors for an extra-decorative spider.

Materials

● About 110 yards (100m) of yarn

● Spool knitter

● Tapestry needle

● Scissors

● Beads, buttons, or sew-on toy eyes

● Cardboard

● Four dishes or jars of different diameters to draw around to make circles for pompom making. Their diameters should be approximately 6 inches (15cm), 3 inches (8cm), 2 inches (5cm), and 1 inch (3cm)

● Darning needle

Making the body

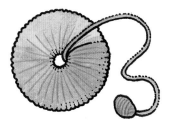

▲ Make a big pompom for the spider's body.

1 A giant pompom is going to be the body of the spider. Cut out two cardboard disks, each with a 6-inch (15cm) outer circle and a 2-inch (5cm) central hole. This will make a nice, fat body for your spider.

2 Wind the yarn around the disks until there is still just enough room to push your finger through the hole in the middle. You could try making a patterned pompom by winding layers of different colored yarns around the disks. Don't cut or tie the pompom yet.

Assembling the pieces

▲ Thread the spool-knitted legs through the hole in the pompom.

1 Thread the four lengths of spool knitting that you made for the spider's legs exactly halfway through the hole in the middle of the pompom.

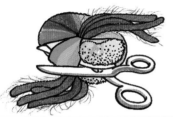

▲ Cut around the cardboard disks.

2 Now carefully cut around the pompom, between the disks. Don't cut the legs.

▲ Tie some strong yarn tightly around the middle of the pompom.

3 Use a strong yarn to tie the pompom securely, trapping the legs into place. Do not trim the ends yet.

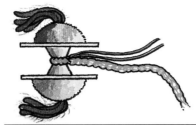

▲ Tie the finger-knitted dangling string around the middle of the pompom.

4 Now tie one end of the finger knitting tightly around the middle of the pompom to fix the dangling string in place.

5 Now you can remove the cardboard disks from the pompom.

Making the head

1 Make a smaller pompom for the spider's head, this time using 3-inch (8cm) disks with 1-inch (3cm) holes.

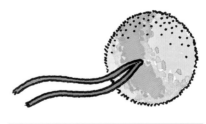

▲ Remove the cardboard disks but don't trim the ties.

2 Cut and tie the pompom with a length of strong yarn and remove the disks. Do not trim the ties yet.

Attaching the head

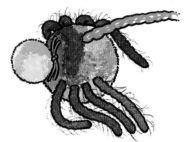

▲ Knot the ties together to join the two pompoms.

1 Join the head and body by knotting together the ties on both pompoms as tightly as you can.

2 Trim the loose ends and, presto, your spider has a head.

Adding eyes

▲ Stitch some eyes onto the spider's head.

1 Dangle your spider to check how it will hang. Using a tapestry needle, stitch two beads, buttons, or sew-on toy eyes into place. Stitch firmly through the middle of the head so that the eyes are held securely.

Now find a cat or other friend—they don't have to be furry!—and start dangling.

Pick up your needles

Now it's time to knit with two needles. In this chapter you will learn how to cast on stitches, how to knit using the basic knit stitch, and how to bind off when you have finished a piece of knitting. All knitting is based on these important skills. The projects that follow the techniques will help you to put your newly learned knitting skills into practice, so what are you waiting for? Pick up your needles and start knitting.

Casting on

Casting on is the process of making your first row of stitches on a knitting needle. There are several different ways of casting on, but making a slip knot is always the first step.

Remember that the working end of the yarn comes from the ball, so the loose end is, of course, the other end.

Making a slip knot

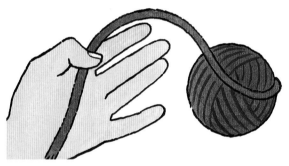

1 Grip the loose end of the yarn between your thumb and hand with your palm facing toward you.

2 Wrap the working end of the yarn right around your first two fingers.

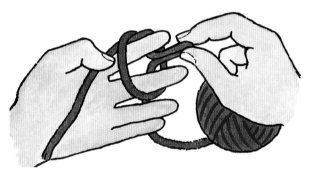

3 Using the finger and thumb of your other hand, reach down into the loop that you have made and pull through the working end of the yarn to form a new loop.

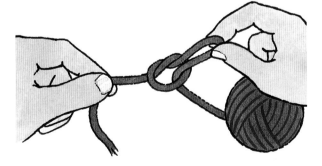

4 Hold this loop with one hand and pull the loose end of the yarn with the other hand. Simple.

You have now made a slip knot.

Simple cast-on

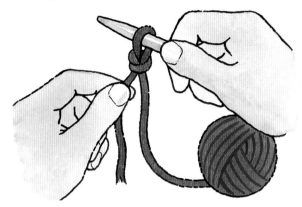

All of the projects in this book tell you exactly how many stitches to cast on, but right now you just need to do about 10 to 20 stitches to practice the techniques.

1 Slide the slip knot onto the knitting needle and gently tighten it. This forms your first stitch.

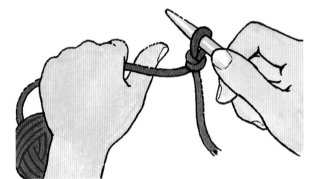

2 Hold the needle in one hand and grip the working end of the yarn with the fingers of your other hand.

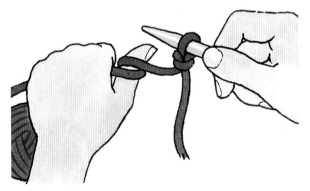

3 Wrap the working end of the yarn around your thumb so that it forms a loop.

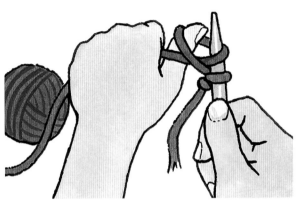

4 Push the tip of the needle up through the loop on your thumb.

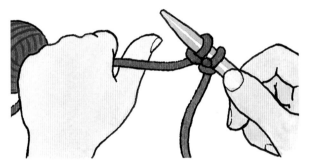

5 Slip your thumb out of the loop and gently pull the working end of the yarn to tighten the new stitch on the needle.

6 Repeat Steps 3–5 until you have around 10 or 20 stitches on the needle, depending on how much practice you want to do.

Tip

When tightening the stitches, make sure that they are still loose enough to slide up and down the needle easily.

Holding the needles and yarn

So far you have worked with only a single needle. To start knitting, you will need to get used to holding two needles and the yarn all at the same time. Just like anything new, it will feel a bit strange at first, but with a bit of practice you will soon get used to it. Cast on about 10 to 20 stitches and you are ready to start.

Holding the needles

When you are about to start knitting, hold the needle with the cast-on stitches in your left hand and hold the empty needle in your right hand.

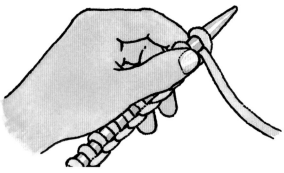

1 Hold your left hand lightly over the top of the needle, gripping the tip of the needle between your thumb and index finger.

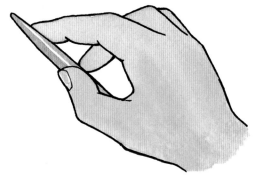

3 Now try holding the empty needle in your right hand like a knife, with your hand over the top of the needle. You can tuck the end of the needle under your arm if your needles are long enough to do this.

2 Take the empty needle in your right hand, holding it like a pencil. The needle should rest on top of your hand between the thumb and index finger.

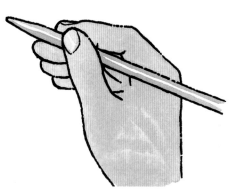

4 Practice pushing the tip of the right-hand needle up into the first stitch on the left-hand needle, from front to back. Try it when you are holding the right-hand needle like a pencil, then try it again holding the right-hand needle like a knife. Which method do you prefer?

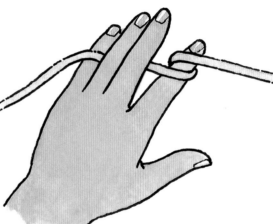

● ●

Holding the yarn

There are several different ways of holding the yarn, but holding it in your right hand is a good way to start. The yarn must be held securely so that your knitting is not too loose. Wrapping the yarn around your fingers gives it "tension," which means that it pulls quite tight as it passes through your hand.

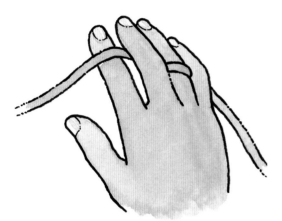

1 Wrap the yarn coming from the first stitch over your right index finger, under your middle finger, over your third finger, and under your little finger. You can now grip the yarn with your little finger to hold it taut.

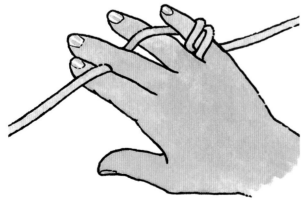

2 If you keep forgetting to grip the yarn with your little finger, you could try wrapping the yarn around your little finger to hold it more firmly.

3 If you are left-handed, you may find it easier to hold the yarn in your left hand. Wrap it around your left index finger, so that it is held taut when you raise your finger. You should still hold the empty needle in your right hand and the needle with the cast-on stitches in your left hand.

4 Practice holding the yarn and the needles at the same time, and you will be able to start knitting.

There are lots of different ways of holding yarn and needles. This book shows two ways of doing it. Neither method is better than the other. It's just important to find the one that suits you, so try both ways and see which one you prefer.

Knit stitch

Now that you know how to hold the yarn and needles and can cast on, you are ready to start knitting. The knit stitch is the most basic stitch used to make knitted fabric and you can use it to make all the projects in this chapter. So let's get going!

In knitting, the stitches are moved from the left-hand needle to the right-hand needle.

1 Cast on about 10 to 20 stitches. Hold the needle with the cast-on stitches in your left hand and hold the empty needle in your right hand.

2 Insert the right-hand needle up into the center of the first stitch so that the two needles cross each other and the right needle is behind the left. Make sure the working end of the yarn is behind the needle, as shown in the picture.

3 Using your index finger, wrap the working end of the yarn from behind the right-hand needle, from left to right, passing the yarn between both needles. If you're holding the yarn in your right hand, it will look like this.

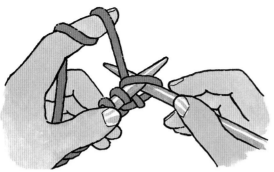

4 If you're holding the yarn in your left hand, make a stitch in exactly the same way, but use your left index finger to wrap the yarn around the needle.

5 Still holding the yarn taut, lower the tip of the right needle down into the center of the stitch and toward you. This will pull a new loop through the stitch.

6 Pull the right needle up so that the stitch on the left needle slips off the top, and the new stitch stays on the right-hand needle. Well done. You now have your first knit stitch on the right needle.

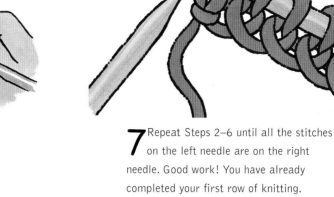

7 Repeat Steps 2–6 until all the stitches on the left needle are on the right needle. Good work! You have already completed your first row of knitting.

8 Now swap the needles so that you are holding the needle with the stitches in your left hand and the empty needle in your right hand. You can now knit the next row, starting again at Step 2. Make sure that the yarn is behind the needles before you start and remember to keep the yarn taut while you knit.

9 Continue until your knitting is as long as you want it to be and you will be ready to bind off.

When you are making the projects, we will tell you exactly how many rows to knit. Here you are practicing, so make as many rows as you need until you feel confident and comfortable with the knit stitch.

Techniques

Finishing the knitting

When you have finished knitting, you need to bind off to make a neat edge that doesn't unravel. You will also need to hide any loose ends of yarn coming from your knitting at the cast-on and bind-off edges. This is called weaving in loose ends and will make your finished work look neat and tidy.

The "wrong side" of the knitting is the side that you won't see when the knitted article is finished—for example, the inside of a sweater.

Binding off

1 Knit the first two stitches as usual at the beginning of the row where you want to bind off.

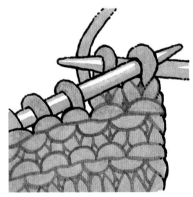

2 Insert the tip of the left needle down into the bottom stitch (the first stitch you made) on the right needle.

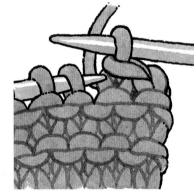

3 Hold the top stitch in place with your right index finger and carefully lift the bottom stitch over the top stitch and off the end of the right-hand needle.

4 Take the left needle out of the stitch, leaving you with one stitch on the right needle.

5 Knit into the next stitch of the row so that you have two stitches on the right needle again.

6 Repeat Steps 2–5 until you have just one stitch remaining on the right needle and no more stitches on the left needle.

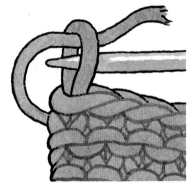

7 Cut the yarn about 4 inches (10cm) from the needle. Thread the end of the yarn through the stitch on the needle and remove the needle. Pull the yarn end to tighten.

Weaving in loose ends

1 When the needles are no longer in the knitting, you will be left with two loose strands of yarn, one at each end of the knitting. Thread the loose strand at the bind-off edge onto a tapestry needle.

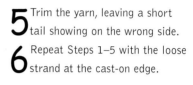

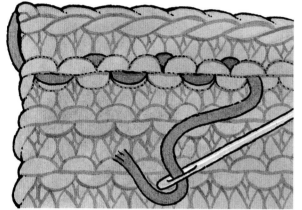

2 On the wrong side of the knitting, stitch under and over the nearest six or seven stitches, following the row along the bind-off edge of the knitting.

3 Stretch the knitting a bit to loosen the woven-in end so that it is not too tight.

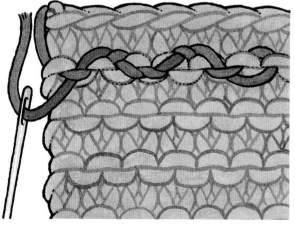

4 Double back, stitching back into the woven-in yarn to make the end really secure.

5 Trim the yarn, leaving a short tail showing on the wrong side.

6 Repeat Steps 1–5 with the loose strand at the cast-on edge.

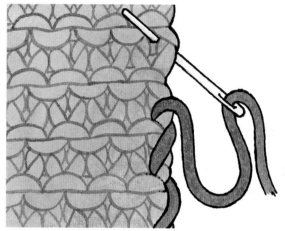

7 If you are knitting something big, you will usually have to use more than one ball of yarn (you'll learn how to do this on page 48). Wherever you've started a new ball, you'll be left with two loose ends of yarn at the edge of your knitting. Weave these into your knitting in the same way as before, but follow the vertical edge of the knitting instead of working along a row.

Can you believe how easy it is to knit? Well, let's start using your new skill to make some fun and useful things.

Funny-face bag

This drawstring bag is easy to make. It's a great way of using up odd balls of yarn and will give you a chance to practice casting on, doing the knit stitch, and binding off. Then you can decorate the bag with stitching, embroidery, and fringe.

If you follow the instructions here, you will make a small bag that can be used as a treasure pouch or purse and doesn't take long to make. If you want to make a bigger bag, you can keep knitting until you've had enough, or until you run out of yarn. The longer you knit, the longer your bag will be. Have fun making a quirky face by adding eyes, a nose, a mouth, and hair. Silly, cute, or ugly, you can't go wrong! You could even try making a whole crazy bag family in different sizes.

You are now going to use the knitting skills you learned on pages 24–31. If you need a reminder of how to do something, just look back to the pictures and instructions there.

Let's get knitting!

Knitting the bag

1 Cast on 30 stitches using the simple cast-on method and worsted-weight yarn.

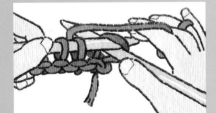

▲ Knit the bag using the knit stitch.

2 Knit each stitch on every row until your piece of knitting is about 12 inches (30cm) long.

3 Bind off and weave in the loose ends of yarn at the bind-off and cast-on edges.

▲ The funny face needs to fit onto one half of the knitting.

4 Fold the knitting in half to find the bottom edge of the bag (this is shown by a dotted line in the picture). Remember that the face needs to fit onto the front of the bag, so think about where you want to position the eyes, nose, and mouth.

5 Use a tapestry needle and other scraps of yarn to sew on a pair of toy eyes or buttons.

Materials

● About 110 yards (100m) of worsted-weight yarn for the bag

- - - - - - - - - -

● Assorted scraps of yarn for the face, hair, and seams

- - - - - - - - - -

● Size 8 (5mm) knitting needles

- - - - - - - - - -

● Scissors

- - - - - - - - - -

● Tapestry needle

- - - - - - - - - -

● Toy eyes or buttons

- - - - - - - - - -

● Length of narrow ribbon, spool knitting, or braid

- - - - - - - - - -

● Crochet hook

- - - - - - - - - -

● Darning needle

Chain-stitch mouth

1 You are now going to use chain stitch and a scrap of yarn to make a smiley mouth. Put a knot in the end of the yarn and thread the other end through a tapestry needle.

2 Start sewing by pushing the needle through the knitting from the wrong side. The side where you've sewn the eyes will be the right side of the bag, so the other side is therefore the wrong side.

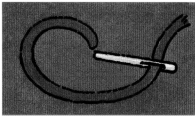
▲ Push the needle back through to the wrong side, leaving a small loop.

3 Push the needle back through the knitting in almost the same place, leaving a loop of thread sticking out.

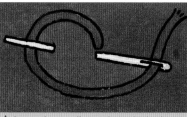
▲ Bring the needle up through the loop to make the first chain stitch.

4 Move the needle along a little to begin the next stitch. Pass the needle through to the front of your knitting, coming up inside the loop you just made. Then push the needle down again through the same place, creating a new loop as you go.

▲ Keep sewing chain stitches to make the mouth.

5 Keep making loop stitches by repeating Steps 2–4 and you will soon see a "chain" of stitching appear. Give him a nice big grin.

● ●

Satin-stitch nose

1 Satin stitch is a different type of stitch that you can use to make a round nose as big or as small as you like. Knot the end of another scrap of yarn and thread the other end through the tapestry needle.

2 Pass the needle through the knitting from the wrong side, then pass it back through the knitting a little farther along to make a small stitch.

3 Now make another slightly bigger stitch just above the first.

▲ Use satin stitch to give your bag a nose.

4 Repeat Steps 2–3, making bigger and then smaller stitches until you have made a round nose just the size that you want. Not only can you knit, but now you know two embroidery stitches as well.

Project 2

Fringe hair

1 To make a woolly fringe for the hair, cut several pieces of scrap yarn about 6 inches (15cm) long. Thick or fluffy yarn will work well.

2 Take two or more pieces and fold them in half to make a loop.

▲ Use a crochet hook to pull a loop of yarn through the edge of the bag.

3 At the cast-on edge of the knitting, starting on one side, push a crochet

hook from the wrong side to the right side (the front of the bag). Use the hook to pull the loop of yarn through from the right side to the wrong side.

▲ Pull the ends of the piece of fringe through the loop.

4 Now use the crochet hook to pull the ends of the yarn through the loop.

▲ Tighten the knot to make the fringe stick out from the top of the bag.

5 Pull the yarn to tighten the knot so that the loose ends stick out like hair.

6 Repeat Steps 2–5 until the cast-on edge is covered in fringe, then do the same thing all along the bind-off edge.

• •

Overcasting the seams

1 Fold the bag in half so that the side seams meet exactly and you can see the face you have made.

2 Thread a darning needle with a yarn that contrasts in color to the knitting, so that it will stand out. Knot one end of the yarn.

▲ Keeping the knot inside the bag, push the needle through to the front.

3 The overcasting method is an easy and decorative way to sew seams. Starting at the bottom corner, make

sure that the knot is on the inside of the bag, and stitch through to the front of the knitting.

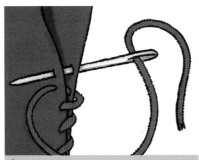

▲ Use overcasting stitch to sew the seam of your bag.

4 Take the yarn over the edge to the back of the bag, a bit farther along, and stitch through both layers to the front. Work along the seam in this way until you get to the top.

▲ Make the seam secure by sewing a double stitch at the end.

5 Do a double stitch at the end to keep the seam from coming undone. Pass the needle through to the inside of the bag and cut the yarn.

6 Now repeat Steps 2–5 on the other side of the bag.

Let's get knitting!

Drawstring

▲ Thread a drawstring around the top of the bag.

1 You can make a drawstring using a length of narrow ribbon, spool knitting, or braid. Using a crochet hook or your fingers, thread the drawstring in and out of the knitted stitches around the top of the bag.

2 Knot the ends of the drawstring, pull tight, and your stuff will be safe!

Now that you've made a funny-face bag, why not make one for your best friend in different colors and with an even funnier face?

Rainbow friendship bands

Choose a rainbow of your best friend's favorite colors to create this striped bracelet and choker. They are so pretty that you will want to make a set for yourself. You could even try making a matching flower, using the instructions for any of the Fantastic Flowers on pages 42–47, to decorate a really special choker.

If you need help with some of the knitting skills used in this project, simply look back to pages 24–31, where all the techniques you will be using are explained.

Seven-stripe bracelet

Arranging the stripes

▲ Try different color combinations until you find one you like.

1 Spend a little time before you start knitting on deciding which colors look best together. Lay out strands of yarn to make the best stripe pattern that you can. The final color will need to be cut to 5 feet (1.5m), and the other colors each need to be 3 feet (1m) long.

Knitting the bracelet

1 Take the first 3-foot (1m) length of yarn and make the cast-on slip knot about 8 inches (20cm) from the beginning of the strand. Cast on 24 stitches using the simple cast-on method.

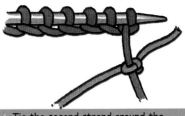

▲ Tie the second strand around the first strand at the beginning of the next row.

2 Now take the second colored strand and tie it in a knot around the first strand of yarn, leaving an 8-inch (20cm) tail before the knot.

3 Slide the knot right up toward the first stitch of the knitting and hold the tail out of your way for the first few stitches. Knit one row using the new yarn.

4 At the end of the row, join the next strand of yarn in the same way and knit one row.

5 Add on the next three colored strands in the same way.

6 Take the final, longer strand of yarn and join it in as usual. Knit one row.

7 Bind off but do not weave in the loose ends.

Striped strands!

Materials

● A selection of different colored fine yarns, such as fingering-weight cotton, glittery crochet thread, or embroidery strands. You will need six 3-foot (1m) lengths and one 5-foot (1.5m) length for the bracelet, and seven 3-foot (1m) lengths and one 7-foot (2m) length for the choker

- - - - - - - - - - - - - -

● Size 6 (4mm) knitting needles

- - - - - - - - - - - - - -

● Scissors

- - - - - - - - - - - - - -

● Masking tape

Braiding the ties

1 Lay the knitted strip on a flat surface and straighten out all the loose ends.

2 Use a piece of masking tape to hold the middle of the strip securely on the surface.

3 Braid all the loose strands at one end of the bracelet for about 2 inches (5cm) to make a tie. If you need a reminder of how to do braiding, look back at page 17.

▲ Tie a knot at the end of the braid and trim it neatly.

4 Knot the end of the braid securely and trim to leave the ends about 1 inch (2cm) long.

5 Repeat Steps 3–4 at the other end of the bracelet.

Now that you have the hang of them, these friendship bands can be knitted in any width. Just use more or fewer stripes.

Eight-stripe choker

1 Design a stripe pattern to coordinate with the bracelet. Remember that the final strand needs to be longer than the rest.

2 Start with a 3-foot (1m) length of yarn. Make the cast-on slip knot about 10 inches (25cm) from the beginning of the yarn and cast on 46 stitches.

3 Tie the second colored strand in a knot around the first strand of yarn, leaving a 10-inch (25cm) tail before the knot.

4 Follow Steps 3–4 of Knitting the Bracelet until you have added in the five remaining 3-foot (1m) lengths of yarn.

5 Take the final, 7-foot (2m) length of colored yarn and join it in as usual. Knit one row.

6 Bind off but do not weave in the loose ends.

7 Braid the ties in the same way as you did for the bracelet, but this time make them about 3 inches (8cm) long.

Mini-knitting pins

You can make this cluster of unusual pins by knitting on tiny, doll-sized needles. When you wear them, all of your friends will be amazed that you can knit so small. The two mini knitting needles are made from small wooden skewers and beads. All you need to do is cast on as usual and knit.

Knitting on tiny needles is exactly the same as using ordinary needles, just much smaller, so you can still refer to pages 24–31 if you need a reminder of how to do something.

Mini-needles pin

This pin consists of a miniature pair of knitting needles and a tiny ball of yarn, so it looks like someone is halfway through a piece of knitting. It's simple to make, takes hardly any time and even less yarn, and you don't need to bind off!

Small is fun!

Making mini needles

1 Choose two small sticks to make the needles. These can be traditional bamboo skewers or you could find colorful plastic versions.

2 Find a pair of beads to form the knobs at the end of each needle. The hole in the bead should be the right size to fit onto the stick.

Dip the stick in some glue, then push it into the hole of the bead.

3 Dip the tip of one stick into a small amount of craft glue and insert it into the hole in one of the beads. Hold the stick and bead together for a few minutes to let the glue set a little.

4 Wipe away any excess glue and allow to dry thoroughly. Repeat for the other needle.

Materials

- At least 7 feet (2m) of fine yarn, such as fingering-weight cotton, crochet thread, or embroidery thread
- 2 small wooden skewers
- 2 beads, about ¼ inch (5-10mm) diameter
- Craft glue
- Scissors
- ¼ x 1 inch (5 x 25mm) strip of paper and some adhesive tape
- Pin with safety clasp or safety pin
- Tapestry needle

Mini knitting

1 Take a fine yarn and cast on ten stitches with the mini needles.

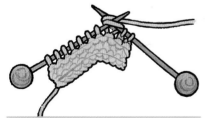

Use your mini needles to knit ten rows.

2 Using the knit stitch on every row, knit ten rows. You will need to have at least 24 inches (60cm) of yarn left.

3 Do not bind off. Leave the knitting on the needle.

4 Put the empty needle safely to one side for the moment.

Making the mini ball of yarn

Wrap the yarn around two of your fingers to make a mini ball of yarn.

1 Cut the yarn so that you have about 24 inches (60cm) left. Starting 2 inches (5cm) from the knitting, wind the yarn loosely around and around two of your fingers, making a mini ball of yarn.

Wrap the end of the yarn tightly around the middle of the ball.

2 Wrap the last 2 inches (5cm) of the yarn firmly around and around the middle of the ball, to hold it tight.

Wrap a strip of paper around the yarn to look like a ball band.

3 Wrap the strip of paper around the tiny ball and use a little bit of adhesive tape to keep it in place. This looks like a ball band and will hold the yarn in place.

Fixing the pin to the clip

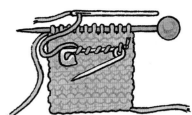

Stitch a backing pin or safety pin to the back of the knitting.

1 The backing pin or safety pin must be fastened near the top of the knitting, on the back. You can use a tapestry needle and some spare yarn to stitch over the pin and into the back of the knitting.

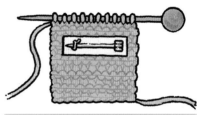

If your pin has a flat surface, you can glue it in place instead.

2 If the pin has a flat surface, you may be able to use craft glue to hold it in place. Whichever method you use, be sure that the pin looks neat from the front.

3 Get the empty needle that you put to one side and push it through the piece of knitting.

Well done! Now you can wear your pin and impress everyone with your great new knitting skills.

Mini knitted hat and scarf pins

Now that you have the hang of miniature knitting, you can make another pair of mini knitting needles and knit this fun pair of pins.

Materials

● About 25 feet (7m) of fine yarn, such as fingering-weight cotton, crochet thread, or embroidery thread

---

● Pair of mini knitting needles, like you made on page 38

● Scissors

● Tapestry needle

● 2 pins with safety clasp or safety pins

Making the scarf

1 On the mini knitting needles, cast on four stitches as usual. Knit 30 rows.

2 Bind off and weave in the ends on the wrong side. The wrong side is the side where you're going to attach the pin when you've finished knitting.

3 Now make the fringe. This is like the fringe on the Funny-face Bag on page 34, but you will need to use a tapestry needle instead of a crochet hook because the stitches are so small. First, cut eight 4-inch (10cm) lengths of fine yarn.

△ Use a tapestry needle to thread fringe through the end of the scarf.

4 Fold a length of yarn in half and thread the folded end through a tapestry needle. Stitch it through the end of the scarf to the wrong side and remove the needle, leaving the yarn in the knitting.

5 Carefully thread the ends of the fringe through the loop and pull to secure.

△ Trim the fringe neatly.

6 Repeat Steps 4–5 to make four fringes at each end of the scarf, then trim the ends.

7 Carefully attach the scarf to a backing pin or safety pin, like you did on page 39.

Making the hat

1 On the mini knitting needles, cast on eight stitches as usual. Leave an 8-inch (20cm) tail of yarn at the beginning of the row.

2 Knit 20 rows. Bind off, but don't weave in the loose ends.

△ Sew a few small stitches to hold the turn-up in place.

3 Thread the tail at the cast-on end onto a tapestry needle and fold the first three rows of knitting up to the right side. The right side is the side that you want to face outward when you're wearing the pin. Make a few tiny stitches into the turn-up to hold it in place.

4 Weave in the loose ends on the wrong side.

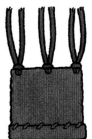

△ Add a tassel at each corner and in the center of the top of the hat.

5 To make a tassel, cut three 8-inch (20cm) lengths of the fine yarn. Use a tapestry needle to make three fringes, like you did in Steps 4–6 of Making the Scarf, one at each corner and one in the center of the bind-off row.

Small is fun!

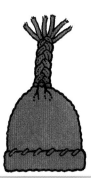

⚠ Braid the tassel and tie a knot at the end to keep the braid secure.

6 Braid the fringe tightly for about ¼ –½ inch (1cm). If you need a reminder of how to do braiding, look back at page 17. The braid will gather in the top of the hat. Tie the ends securely with a double knot, then trim the ends evenly.

7 Carefully attach the hat to a backing pin or safety pin, like you did on page 39.

You could also make mini-knitting barrettes that will look great in your hair.

Fantastic flowers

Make bouquets of these amazing knitted pins and you can use them to decorate sweaters, bags, or bedrooms. This is a chance to experiment with sparkly, fancy yarns and fluffy mohair, and to add on sequins and beads. The more exotic, the more colorful, the better!

To make these flowers, you will be using the skills you learned on pages 24–31, so you can always look again at the instructions and pictures there if you need a little extra help.

Giant mohair flower

This is a really fun way to make your first flower. It is knitted in fluffy mohair yarn and decorated with sequins and a giant bead.

Something sparkly!

Knitting the flower

1 Cast on 40 stitches. Knit each stitch on every row for 12 rows.

2 Bind off, leaving a tail of yarn about 8 inches (20cm) long.

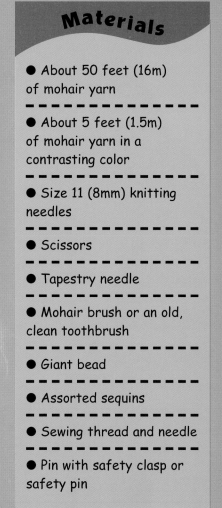

Materials

● About 50 feet (16m) of mohair yarn

● About 5 feet (1.5m) of mohair yarn in a contrasting color

● Size 11 (8mm) knitting needles

● Scissors

● Tapestry needle

● Mohair brush or an old, clean toothbrush

● Giant bead

● Assorted sequins

● Sewing thread and needle

● Pin with safety clasp or safety pin

Running stitch

1 Thread a tapestry needle with the tail of yarn.

2 You now need to gather the center of the flower using a running stitch. This is an easy way of gathering up knitting. Push the needle down through the last stitch of the bind-off edge.

3 Now skip a stitch and bring the needle back up through the next stitch of the bind-off edge.

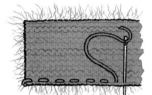

▲ Sew a running stitch along the bind-off edge of your knitting.

4 Stitch all along the edge in the same way, pushing the needle into every other stitch.

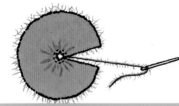

▲ Pull one end of the yarn to gather the knitting into a circle shape.

5 When you get to the end of the row, gently pull the yarn through until the bind-off edge is completely gathered up.

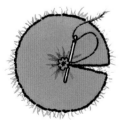

▲ Sew a few stitches through the center to hold the circle in place.

6 Stitch back through the gathered knitting to secure the thread.

Sewing the seam

1 The gathered edge will be the center of the flower. Bring the two open sides of the knitting to meet each other and make a circular flower shape.

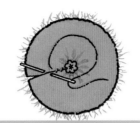

▲ Use overcasting stitch to sew the open edge of the circle closed.

2 Using the thread already on the needle, stitch the open sides of the flower together. You can use a small overcasting stitch to do this, as we did on page 34 with the Funny-face Bag. Sew the seam on the wrong side of the flower.

3 Weave in the loose ends on the wrong side.

Brushing the mohair

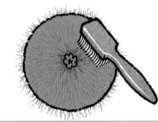

▲ Gently brush the mohair to make it more fluffy.

1 Mohair always looks much fluffier if it is brushed after being knitted. Using a mohair brush or an old, clean toothbrush, gently brush the front of the knitting from the center of the flower out to the edge.

Embroidering the loopy center

1 The loopy stitch center of this flower looks really good if it is stitched with mohair yarn in a color that contrasts with the main flower. Thread a tapestry needle with about 4½ feet (1.5m) of yarn and knot the ends together so you have a double strand.

2 Pull the needle and thread through a stitch near the center of the flower from the back to the front.

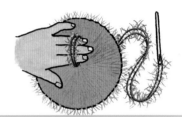

▲ Wrap the yarn around three of your fingers to make a loop.

3 Place three fingers in the center of the flower. Pass the yarn over your fingers and stitch back down through the center of the flower, forming a loop of yarn over your fingers. Slip your fingers out of the loop.

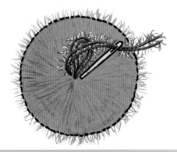

▲ Make a small stitch to secure the loop to the center of the flower.

4 Bring the needle back through to the front and make a small stitch through to the back. This will secure the loop.

5 Repeat Steps 2–4 to make five more loops.

6 Sew a double stitch with the yarn at the back of the flower to secure it, then cut the yarn.

Something sparkly!

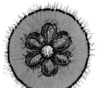

Decorating the flower

▲ Sew a giant bead in the center of the flower.

1 Put a giant bead in the center of the flower and sew it in place. You will probably need to use ordinary sewing thread and a sewing needle at this stage, because the yarn and tapestry needle will both be too thick.

2 A few carefully placed sequins can transform plain knitting. You can choose a sewing thread to match either the sequins or the knitting, or go for a gold or silver thread for something very decorative. Thread the sewing needle and tie a knot in the other end of the thread.

3 Decide where you want to put the sequin. Stitch up from the back of the knitting, passing the needle through a strand of yarn so the knot holds.

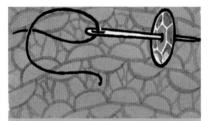

▲ Thread the needle through a sequin.

4 Pass the needle through the hole in the sequin.

5 Slide the sequin down the thread until it touches the knitting.

▲ Let the thread go over the top of the sequin and stitch through to the back.

6 Pass the thread over the sequin and stitch back into the knitting just behind the sequin.

7 Bring the thread back up through the hole in the sequin and back down into the knitting on the other side of the sequin.

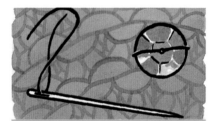

▲ Bring the needle to the front where you want to sew another sequin.

8 Get ready to sew the next sequin in place and bring the needle through to the front of the knitting in the position you have chosen.

9 Repeat Steps 4–8 until you have sewn on all the sequins. Make a few tight stitches into the back of your knitting to secure the thread, then trim it.

10 Now that you have finished the flower, attach it to a backing pin or safety pin like you did with the Mini-knitting Pins on page 39.

Rosette flower

This flower uses two different colored glittery crochet threads. Choose colors that you think look exciting together and decorate the flower with sequins to make it even more sparkly.

Outside rosette

1 Take the first color of glittery crochet thread and cast on 14 stitches. Knit 120 rows.

2 Bind off, leaving a 1-foot (30cm) tail of yarn. Thread the yarn onto a tapestry needle.

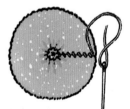

▲ Sew a running stitch along one edge and pull it tight to form a circle.

3 Gather up the long edge of the knitting using a running stitch, like you did on page 43 with the Giant Mohair Flower.

▲ Stitch the open edge of the circle shape closed.

4 Stitch the cast-on and bind-off ends of the strip together using a small overcasting stitch on the back of the flower.

5 Weave in the ends of the yarn on the back of the flower.

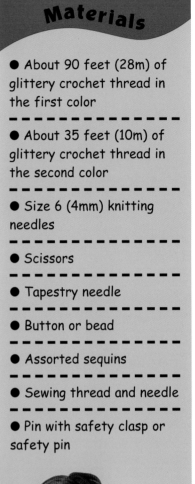

Materials

- About 90 feet (28m) of glittery crochet thread in the first color
- About 35 feet (10m) of glittery crochet thread in the second color
- Size 6 (4mm) knitting needles
- Scissors
- Tapestry needle
- Button or bead
- Assorted sequins
- Sewing thread and needle
- Pin with safety clasp or safety pin

Center rosette

1 Now take the second color of glittery crochet thread and cast on eight stitches. Knit 70 rows.

2 Bind off, leaving a 1-foot (30cm) tail of yarn. Thread the yarn onto a tapestry needle.

3 Gather and stitch just as you did in Steps 3–5 of knitting the Outside Rosette.

Assembling the flower

1 Place the smaller rosette in the center of the larger rosette.

▲ Stitch the small rosette onto the center of the large rosette.

2 Take some more of the crochet thread you used for the small rosette and thread about 1 foot (30cm) onto a tapestry needle. Stitch the two rosettes together close to the center, ending with the needle at the back of the flower. Make a few small stitches to secure.

3 Thread the needle through the very center of the flower from back to front and sew on a button or bead. If the needle doesn't fit through the hole in the button or bead, you may need to use a sewing needle and thread for this stage.

4 Decorate the rosette with sequins, like you did with the Giant Mohair Flower on page 44. Then you can fix it to a backing pin or safety pin. Look back at page 39 of the Mini-knitting Pins project to see how to do this.

Just look at the fantastic flower you have made. Did you ever think you could make such cool things with knitting?

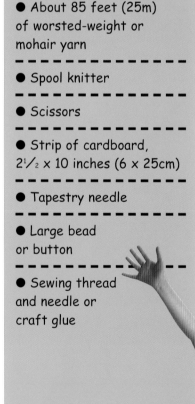

Loopy flower

This flower is made using a long piece of spool knitting. A fine mohair will work well, but you can experiment with other kinds of yarn, such as worsted-weight yarn.

1 Make a 4-foot (120cm) length of spool knitting. Look back at page 15 if you need a reminder of how to do this. Bind off the end, leaving a tail of yarn about 1 foot (30cm) long.

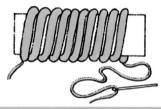

▲ Wrap your length of spool knitting around the strip of cardboard.

2 Position one end of the spool knitting at the bottom edge of the strip of cardboard. Wrap the knitting around and along the cardboard strip, making ten loops and finishing with the other end of the knitting at the bottom of the cardboard. Thread the tail of yarn onto a tapestry needle.

3 Lay the cardboard on a flat surface to hold the knitting in position. Push the loops close together.

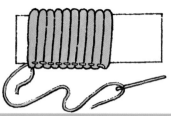

▲ Stitch through each of the loops on the cardboard.

4 Stitch through the first loop of knitting and pass the needle through the knitting of all the remaining loops, working along the bottom edge of the cardboard and finishing with the cast-on end of the knitting.

5 Remove the cardboard and pull the yarn tight, gathering all the loops together.

6 Stitch back into the first loop so that you have made a loopy flower shape.

▲ Sew a few stitches through the center to secure the flower shape.

7 Secure the flower shape by stitching a few times into the center. Weave in the ends of the yarn and trim them.

8 Stitch a bead or button into the center of the flower. You will probably need to use ordinary sewing thread and a sewing needle at this stage, since the yarn and tapestry needle will both be too thick.

9 Attach the flower to a backing pin or safety pin like you did with the Mini-knitting Pins on page 39.

Materials

- About 85 feet (25m) of worsted-weight or mohair yarn
- Spool knitter
- Scissors
- Strip of cardboard, 2¹/₂ x 10 inches (6 x 25cm)
- Tapestry needle
- Large bead or button
- Sewing thread and needle or craft glue

Now that you know how easy it is to make flowers, you can combine
different techniques and yarns to create your own inventions.
What about a loopy mohair flower with a small, sparkly rosette center?

Supersize scarf

This scarf may be big, but you will be amazed at how quickly you can knit it. In contrast to the tiny pin on page 40, but using the same basic knit stitch, this scarf is knitted on big needles with big yarn. You can personalize it with your own name written in huge letters from a length of spool or finger knitting, or you could sew shapes such as hearts and stars onto the scarf instead. It would even look pretty without any extra decoration.

The knitting skills you learned on pages 24–31 are used in this project, so refer to the instructions and pictures there if you have forgotten anything.

Huge and huggable!

Beginning the scarf

1 Cast on 18 stitches with the main, extra-bulky yarn. Knit each stitch in every row. Remember to keep the working end of the yarn taut while you are knitting. The scarf is a great project for practicing how to do this because it's so big. Look back at pages 26–29 if you need a reminder.

2 Continue knitting rows of knit stitch until your ball of yarn is about to run out.

Starting a new ball of yarn

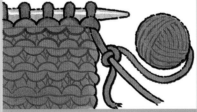

Knot the new yarn around the old yarn at the beginning of a row.

1 You will need to start a new ball of yarn when the one you are using is about to run out or if you want to change to a different color (for example, when knitting stripes). Always try to start a new ball of yarn at the beginning of a row, because it is more difficult to get a neat join in the middle of a row. Cut the yarn that you are finishing, leaving a tail of about 4 inches (10cm). Tie the new yarn around the tail.

2 Slide the knot up close to the knitting, then tighten the knot. Begin knitting with the new ball of yarn that you have just joined in.

More knitting

1 Continue knitting rows of knit stitch until your scarf is about 5 feet (1.5m) long, or as long as you want it to be, if you have enough yarn. If you want, you can just keep knitting and knitting!

2 Bind off, but be especially careful not to bind off too tightly when knitting with this extra-bulky yarn. Make sure the bind-off edge is as loose and stretchy as the giant knitting.

3 Weave all the loose strands of yarn coming from the scarf into the wrong side. Remember to weave in the loose strands from where you started a new ball.

Materials

● 220 yards (200m) of extra-bulky yarn for the scarf

- - - - - - - - - - -

● Yarn in a contrasting color for the letters. You will need about 55 yards (50m) of extra-bulky yarn for a short name like the one shown in this project, or up to 110 yards (100m) of a fine yarn such as fingering-weight cotton for a longer name

- - - - - - - - - - -

● Either 35 yards (30m) of extra-bulky yarn or 90 yards (80m) of fine yarn for the fringe, depending on which you prefer

- - - - - - - - - - -

● Size 19 (15mm) knitting needles

- - - - - - - - - - -

● Scissors

- - - - - - - - - - -

● Tapestry needle

- - - - - - - - - - -

● Spool knitter

- - - - - - - - - - -

● Crochet hook

- - - - - - - - - - -

● Cardboard, about 5 inches (12cm) square

- - - - - - - - - - -

● Pins

"Garter stitch" is a term you may come across as you do more knitting. It simply means that every row is stitched with the knit stitch. So, this scarf has been made in garter stitch.

Picking up dropped garter stitches

If you accidentally drop a stitch while you are knitting, don't worry. You can pick it up and no one will ever know. Try to pick up a dropped stitch as soon as possible or it will keep running farther down.

Use your left needle to lift the dropped stitch over the strand.

3 Use the point of your left needle to lift the dropped stitch over the strand and drop it off the right needle, like binding off. The new stitch is now on the right needle.

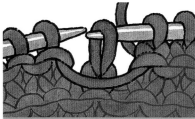

Put the right needle through the dropped stitch from back to front.

1 Put the tip of the right needle through the dropped stitch, going from back to front.

Slip the new stitch onto your left needle and knit it in the usual way.

4 Insert the point of the left needle into the new stitch from front to back and slip the stitch onto the left needle, ready to be knitted as usual.

Put the right needle under the strand from back to front.

2 Insert the tip of the right needle under the strand, going from back to front.

Writing your name

1 You can use either spool knitting or finger knitting to write your name. Look back at pages 14–15 to remind yourself how to do this. If the yarn you are using is fine, you can make strips of spool knitting. If it is bulky, you can use finger knitting instead.

2 You will need to use strips of knitting to make up each element of the letters. For example, the letter T needs two strips—one for the vertical line and one for the horizontal line that goes across the top. Practice writing on the scarf with strands of yarn to see how long each strip needs to be.

3 Make strips of finger or spool knitting the right length for each letter of your name. Remember to bind off at the end of each piece so that it will not unravel.

▲ Pin the strips onto the scarf to form the letters of your name.

4 Lay the scarf on a flat surface and pin the strips into place to make your name. Adjust the positioning until you are happy with how it looks.

Slip stitching the writing into place

1 Slip stitch is often used for sewing one piece of knitting on top of another because the stitching will not be seen from the outside. Thread a tapestry needle with a spare piece of the yarn used for the writing. Make a knot at the end of the yarn.

2 Starting at the beginning of the first letter, gently lift the edge of the strip of spool knitting or finger knitting.

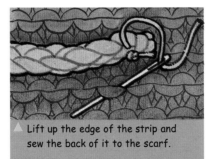

▲ Lift up the edge of the strip and sew the back of it to the scarf.

3 Make a stitch into the back of the strip and take the needle down and through the loop of the nearest stitch on the front of the scarf. Do not stitch right through to the wrong side of the scarf, and make sure that you do not pull the stitches too tight.

4 Bring the needle back up through the knitting, catch it into another stitch on the back of the strip, and down to the nearest stitch on the scarf.

5 Follow Steps 3–4 to continue attaching the underside of the strip to the scarf.

▲ Stitch all along each length of spool or finger knitting.

6 Repeat Steps 2–5 to attach each strip for every letter. At the end of each strip, secure the stitching by sewing twice into the last stitch. Weave in the strands of yarn so that they are hidden.

Huge and huggable!

Making the fringe

1 Your scarf is nearly finished. All you need to do is add some decorative fringe at both ends. You could use the same color as the scarf or the writing, or mix them together. You can use a piece of cardboard to help you measure the lengths of fringe really evenly. About 5 inches (12cm) square is a good size, but you can experiment with longer or shorter fringe if you wish. Wrap the yarn around and around the cardboard.

▲ Cut through the yarn along one edge of the cardboard to make the fringe.

2 Cut in a straight line across the lengths of yarn at one edge of the cardboard, so that you make a pile of strands all the same length.

3 Add fringe to both ends of your scarf, as you did for the Funny-face Bag on page 34.

This is the biggest thing that you have knitted so far. Your supersize scarf is now ready to wear.

Making shapes

You've knitted some fabulous things already, but all your knitting has been square or rectangular. It's now time to learn how to make different shapes by increasing and decreasing stitches. Increasing means adding stitches to make your fabric wider; decreasing means taking stitches away to make your fabric narrower. You can try out these shaping techniques to make a wobbly fried egg, a curved belt, and a triangular headscarf.

Increasing

Increasing is a technique that shapes the knitting by adding stitches. You add stitches to make your knitting wider. There are several different ways to increase. The method you use will depend on how many stitches you want to add and where you want to add them. The cable method is the simplest way of adding one or more extra stitches at the beginning of a row. The bar increase method is good for adding a single stitch anywhere on a row.

Remember that the "working end" of the yarn is the end that comes from the ball.

Cable increase

The cable increase can be used only at the beginning of a row. You can use it to add one or more stitches.

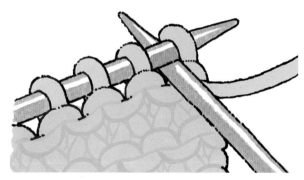

1 Insert the tip of the right-hand needle between the first two stitches on the left-hand needle.

2 Using your index finger, wrap the working end of the yarn from behind the right-hand needle, from left to right, passing the yarn between both needles.

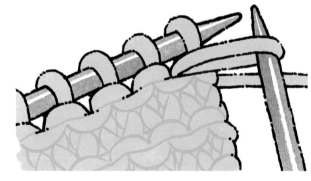

3 Draw a loop through with the right-hand needle.

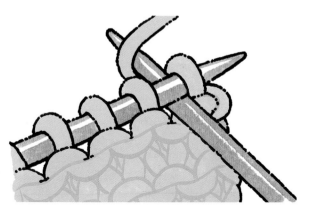

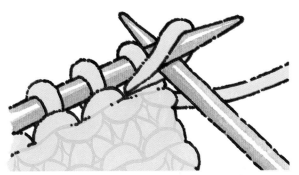

4 Place the new loop on the left needle. You have now increased by one stitch.

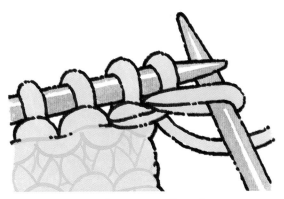

5 Repeat Steps 1–4 until you have increased the right amount of stitches, and continue to knit the row.

Bar increase

The bar increase can be used anywhere in a row, beginning, middle, or end. This increase can add only one stitch.

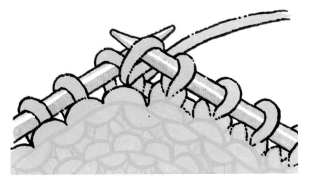

1 Knit into the stitch where you want to increase in the usual way, but do not drop this stitch off the left-hand needle.

3 Knit the stitch again so that you now have two stitches on the right needle.

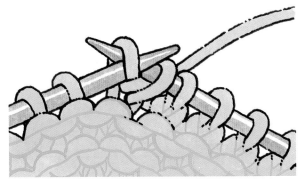

2 Insert the tip of the right-hand needle into the back of the same stitch on the left-hand needle.

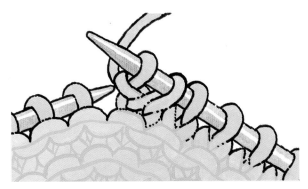

4 Drop the original stitch off the left needle. You have now increased by one stitch and can continue to knit the row.

Decreasing

Decreasing is the method used to shape the knitting by taking stitches away. You decrease stitches to make your knitting narrower. The easiest way to decrease one stitch at a time is to knit two stitches together. You can do this at the beginning, middle, or end of a row. If you need to decrease more than one stitch at the beginning of a row, you will need to use the bind-off method, which you will recognize from binding off. Look back at the instructions for binding off on page 30 to remind yourself how to do this.

Knit 2 together decrease

The knit 2 together decrease can be used anywhere in the row, beginning, middle, or end. It is used to decrease just one stitch.

1 Insert the right needle into two stitches on the left needle instead of one.

2 Knit the two stitches together as if they were one. You have now decreased one stitch and can continue to knit the row.

Now that you are getting more confident with your knitting and know how to make shapes, you can start to learn about knitting patterns and how they look. The projects in this chapter will be written a little more like patterns.

Bind-off decrease

The bind-off decrease can be used only to decrease stitches at the beginning of a row. You can use it to decrease one or more stitches.

1 Knit two stitches at the beginning of the row where you want to decrease.

2 Use the tip of the left needle to lift the bottom stitch on the right-hand needle (the first stitch you made) over the top stitch (the second stitch you made).

3 Knit into the next stitch of the row, then repeat Step 2 to decrease another stitch. Continue until you have decreased the right amount of stitches, then continue to knit the rest of the row.

Cable cast-on

Now that you've learned how to do the cable increase, you can also try a new way of casting on. The cable cast-on method uses both needles and gives a neater edge than the simple cast-on technique you've been using so far.

1 Make a slip knot and put it onto your left needle. Insert the tip of your right needle up into the slip knot so that the needles cross each other and the right needle is behind the left needle.

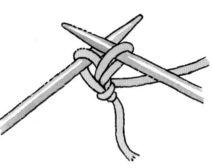

3 Keeping the yarn taut, lower the tip of the right needle down into the center of the slip knot and toward you. This will pull a new loop through the slip knot.

5 Insert the tip of the right needle between the two stitches. Wind the yarn around the right needle like you did in Step 2.

2 Using your index finger, wrap the working end of the yarn from behind the right-hand needle, from left to right, passing the yarn between both needles.

4 Slip the loop onto the left needle, sliding it off the right needle and gently pulling the yarn to secure the stitch.

6 Draw a loop through with the right needle, like in Step 3, and place the new loop on the left needle, like in Step 4.

7 Repeat Steps 5–6, inserting the right needle between the two stitches nearest the tip of the left needle, until you have cast on enough stitches.

When you are making a project, the instructions will tell you how many stitches you need to cast on. To practice, however, around 10 to 20 stitches will be enough.

Sunny-side up

For a fun and easy way to practice increasing and decreasing stitches, knit a fried egg just how you like it—sunny-side up! Choose white and yellow yarn and follow the instructions to create a lifelike wobbly fried egg. You can throw it at your friends or sew it as a patch, but just don't eat it!

To make this fried egg, you will be using all the increasing and decreasing techniques you learned on pages 54–56 as well as the cable cast-on method explained on page 57. You will also continue using the knitting skills learned on pages 24–31. If you need a reminder of how to do something, just flip back to the pictures and instructions there.

Materials

- 25 yards (20m) of yellow worsted-weight yarn
- 45 yards (40m) of white worsted-weight yarn
- Size 8 (5mm) knitting needles
- Scissors
- Tapestry needle
- Small ball of stuffing or cotton
- Pins

Starting the yolk

1 Cast on six stitches using the yellow yarn and the cable cast-on method.

2 **Row 1:** Knit all of the stitches on the first row.

Let's get cooking!

Use a pencil and paper to help keep count of your rows.

Increasing the yolk

You are now going to practice using the bar increase method of adding stitches.

1 Row 2: At the beginning of Row 2, increase one stitch using the bar increase method on the first stitch. Knit the next four stitches, then increase one stitch using the bar increase method on the last stitch. You now have eight stitches on your needle.

2 Rows 3–4: Knit all eight stitches on both these rows.

3 Row 5: At the beginning of Row 5, increase one stitch using the bar increase method on the first stitch. Knit the next six stitches. Increase one stitch using the bar increase method on the last stitch. You now have ten stitches.

4 Rows 6–9: Knit the next four rows. You have now knitted nine rows.

5 Row 10: At the beginning of Row 10, increase one stitch using the bar increase method on the first stitch. Knit the next eight stitches. Increase one stitch using the bar increase method on the last stitch. You now have 12 stitches.

6 Rows 11–18: Knit the next eight rows. Well done. You have already knitted 18 rows and it's time to start decreasing.

Decreasing the yolk

You are going to practice the knit 2 together method to decrease the stitches on the yolk.

1 Row 19: At the beginning of Row 19, knit the first two stitches together. Knit the next eight stitches.

Knit the last two stitches together. You now have ten stitches.

2 Rows 20–23: Knit all ten stitches on the next four rows.

3 Row 24: At the beginning of Row 24, knit the first two stitches together. Knit the next six stitches. Knit the last two stitches together. You now have eight stitches on your needle.

4 Rows 25–26: Knit all of the stitches on the next two rows.

5 Row 27: At the beginning of Row 27, knit the first two stitches together. Knit the next four stitches. Knit the last two stitches together. You now have six stitches.

6 Row 28: Knit all stitches on the next row. Bind off.

Congratulations! The yolk is ready. What a great shape. Now let's knit the egg white.

● ●

Starting the egg white

1 Cast on nine stitches using white yarn and the cable cast-on method.

2 Row 1: Knit all of the stitches on the first row.

Increasing the egg white

You are about to practice the cable increase method of adding stitches.

1 Row 2: At the beginning of Row 2, increase two stitches using the cable increase method. Knit to the end of the row. You now have 11 stitches.

2 Row 3: Knit all of the stitches on the third row.

3 Row 4: At the beginning of Row 4, increase two stitches using the cable increase method. Knit to the end of the row. You now have 13 stitches.

4 Row 5: Knit all of the stitches on the fifth row.

5 Rows 6–10: Increase one stitch at the beginning of each row using

the cable increase method. Knit to the end of each row. You will now have 18 stitches.

6 Row 11: At the beginning of Row 11, increase two stitches using the cable increase method. Knit to the end of the row.

7 Row 12: At the beginning of Row 12, increase one stitch using the cable increase method. Knit to the end of the row.

8 Row 13: At the beginning of Row 13, increase two stitches using the cable increase method. Knit to the end of the row. You can probably now see the wobbly shape being made by

sometimes increasing by one stitch and other times increasing by two stitches.

9 Row 14: At the beginning of Row 14, increase one stitch using the cable increase method. Knit to the end of the row. You now have 24 stitches.

10 Rows 15–25: Knit all of the stitches on the next 11 rows.

11 Rows 26–28: Increase one stitch at the beginning of each row using the cable increase method. Knit to the end of each row. You now have 27 stitches.

12 Rows 29–40: Knit all of the stitches on the next 12 rows.

Let's get cooking!

Decreasing the *egg white*

We are now ready to start decreasing the egg white. This time we will use the bind-off decrease to reduce stitches.

1 Row 41: At the beginning of Row 41, decrease one stitch using the bind-off decrease method. Knit to the end of the row.

2 Rows 42–45: Knit all of the stitches on the next four rows.

3 Rows 46–54: Decrease one stitch at the beginning of each row using the bind-off decrease method.

Knit to the end of each row. You now have 17 stitches.

4 Rows 55–56: Decrease two stitches at the beginning of each row using the bind-off decrease method. Knit to the end of each row. You now have 13 stitches.

5 Rows 57–58: Decrease three stitches at the beginning of each row using the bind-off decrease method. Knit to the end of each row.

6 Bind off all seven remaining stitches of the egg white.

Fantastic work! You have knitted a wobbly egg white. Now let's sew the yolk onto the white.

Assembling the fried egg

1 Lay the wobbly egg white on a flat surface and decide where to position the yolk.

2 Put a small ball of stuffing or cotton behind the yolk. This will make it bulge realistically.

3 Pin the yolk in place, making sure that the stuffing is hidden from view.

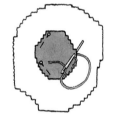

▲ Sew the yolk to the center of the egg white with an overcasting stitch.

4 Thread a tapestry needle with 12 inches (30cm) of leftover yellow yarn, and use a small overcasting stitch, like you did with the Funny-face Bag on page 34, to stitch the yolk neatly into place.

5 Neaten all the loose ends by weaving them in with the tapestry needle.

Now that your fried egg is ready, only you can decide what to do with it. You could stitch it onto a knitted scarf or bag, using white yarn and overcasting stitch.

Or is the floppy Frisbee going to become the next playground craze?

Alternately, you could serve up a knitted fried egg as a practical joke on April Fool's Day!

Desert island belt and headscarf

This project is knitted in soft, natural colored cotton yarn or string, with wooden beads and braided ties. The use of odd-sized needles and knotting creates a trendy, handcrafted macramé effect. You could try using parrot-colored cottons and sparkly beads for a psychedelic paradise island version.

This time you will be using the bar increase and the knit 2 together decrease techniques to shape your fabric. Look back at the pictures and instructions on pages 54–56 if you are not sure how to do the techniques. We will also continue using the knitting skills learned on pages 24–31 and 57.

Wavy belt

To make the curvy shape of the belt, you simply repeat a basic pattern of decreasing and increasing stitches.

Starting the belt

1 Cast on ten stitches using the cable cast-on technique.

2 Knit the first six rows using knit stitch on every row.

Materials

- 45 yards (40m) of worsted-weight cotton yarn

- Size 8 (5mm) knitting needles

- Scissors

- Tapestry needle

- Crochet hook

- 72 wooden beads with holes big enough to thread the cotton yarn through

Curvy shaping

1 You are going to begin shaping the belt using the knit 2 together decrease. At the beginning of the next row, knit the first two stitches together, making the two stitches into one stitch. Now knit the next two stitches together in the same way. Continue to knit two stitches together all along the row so that you finish with five stitches on the right-hand needle.

2 Knit the next eight rows without decreasing any stitches.

3 You are now going to increase the number of stitches again. At the beginning of the next row, increase one stitch using the bar increase method on the first stitch.

Now use the same bar increase method on each stitch of the row. You now have ten stitches on the right needle.

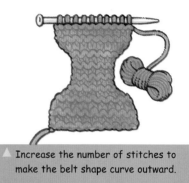

▲ Increase the number of stitches to make the belt shape curve outward.

4 Knit the next six rows without increasing any stitches.

You will see that the pattern of decreasing and increasing is what makes the wavy shape of the belt. It couldn't be easier.

Making the belt the right length

▲ Do enough curvy shapes so that the belt is long enough to fit around your waist.

1 You need to continue knitting to this pattern, following Steps 1–4 of Curvy Shaping, until the belt is just the right length. To make a belt that will fit a 24–28-inch (60–70cm) waist, repeat the decrease and increase shaping five more times. If you want to make the belt to fit a smaller person, measuring 20–24 inches (50–60cm), knit just four more shapings. Or, to fit a larger

person, measuring 28–32 inches (70–80cm), knit six more shapings.

2 Bind off all ten stitches, weave in the loose ends, and trim.

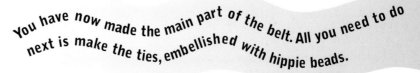

You have now made the main part of the belt. All you need to do next is make the ties, embellished with hippie beads.

Braided ties

1 Cut nine 32-inch (80cm) lengths of cotton yarn. Fold each length in half and use them to make fringes evenly spaced along the edge of the cast-on row, just like you did for the Funny-face Bag on page 34.

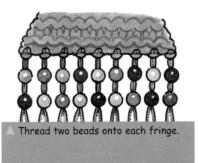

▲ Thread two beads onto each fringe.

2 Thread two beads onto each of the nine fringes of yarn.

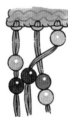

▲ Push a bead up the right-hand fringe and start braiding.

3 Make a braid with the first three fringes (six strands of yarn). If you need a reminder, look at braiding on page 17. You need to push the beads up the fringe one by one so that they become worked into the braid. Start by pushing one bead to the top of the right-hand fringe, then move the rest of the right fringe over to the middle.

▲ Push a bead up the left-hand fringe and continue braiding.

4 Now push one bead to the top of the left-hand fringe, then move the rest of the left fringe over to the middle.

▲ Push a bead up the new right-hand fringe and continue to braid.

5 Push one bead up the new right-hand fringe as far as the crossover point (this is the point where another fringe of yarn crosses over it), then move this fringe over to the middle.

▲ Push another bead up the left-hand fringe and keep braiding.

6 Push a bead up the left-hand fringe to the crossover point, then move the left fringe over to the middle.

▲ Push another bead up the right-hand fringe and keep braiding.

7 Push a bead up the right-hand fringe as far as the crossover point, then move the right fringe over to the middle.

▲ Push the final bead up the left-hand fringe and finish braiding.

8 Push the final bead up the left-hand fringe to the crossover point, then move the left fringe over to the middle.

▲ Separate the strands into two halves and tie a knot below the beads.

9 When all six beads are braided in, divide the six strands of yarn into two groups of three, and tie in a knot to secure the braid.

10 Now braid the next three fringes in the same way and secure with a knot. Then braid the final three fringes in the same way and secure these with a knot.

Castaway fashion!

△ Make two braids with the rest of the yarn.

11 Divide the strands of yarn below the three knots into two halves and braid each half for 6 inches (15cm), tying the end of each braid with a knot to secure.

△ Push a bead onto the end of each strand of yarn, tie a knot, and trim.

12 Now thread a bead onto each individual strand of yarn and tie a double knot below it to keep the bead from falling off. Trim the yarn ends.

You have finished one end of the belt, and doesn't it look funky? Now make the decorative braids at the other end in exactly the same way.

Castaway headscarf

This headscarf uses a combination of thick and thin knitting needles to make loose knitted stripes, using the knit stitch that you have been practicing.

Starting the headscarf

1 Cast on 50 stitches using the cable cast-on technique and size 8 (5mm) knitting needles.

2 Rows 1–2: Work the first two rows in knit stitch.

Materials

● 45 yards (40m) of worsted-weight cotton yarn

● Size 8 (5mm) knitting needles

● One size 19 (15mm) knitting needle

● Scissors

● Tapestry needle

● Crochet hook

● 12 wooden beads with holes big enough to thread the cotton yarn through

Shaping the headscarf

1 You are going to use the knit 2 together decrease to shape the scarf.
Row 3: At the beginning of Row 3, knit the first two stitches together. Knit to the last two stitches, then knit the last two stitches together. You have decreased two stitches and now have 48 stitches on the needle.

2 Row 4: Decrease at both ends of the row as in Row 3, leaving 46 stitches.

▲ Knit the next row using the large needle to make big, loose stitches.

3 Row 5: This row is referred to as the loose row. Put down the empty size 8 (5mm) knitting needle and use the big size 19 (15mm) needle to knit this row. Decrease at both ends of the row as before, leaving 44 stitches.

4 Row 6: Using the size 8 (5mm) needle, knit this row, decreasing at both ends of the row as before, leaving 42 stitches when you have finished.

5 Rows 7–9: Put down the size 19 (15mm) needle and use both size 8 (5mm) needles to knit three rows, decreasing at both ends of each row. You will now have 36 stitches and nine rows.

6 Row 10: Now it's time for another loose row. Knit this row like Row 5, using the size 19 (15mm) needle and decreasing at both ends. You will now have 34 stitches.

7 Rows 11–14: Repeat Rows 6–9, always decreasing at both ends of each row. You will now have 26 stitches.

8 Row 15: This is another loose row. Knit this row like Row 5, using the size 19 (15mm) needle and decreasing at both ends. You will be left with 24 stitches.

9 Rows 16–19: Repeat Rows 6–9 again, always decreasing at both ends of each row. You will now have 16 stitches left.

10 Row 20: You've guessed it, another loose row. Knit this row like Row 5, using the size 19 (15mm) needle and decreasing at both ends, leaving 14 stitches.

11 Row 21: Using the size 8 (5mm) needle, knit this row, decreasing at both ends of the row as before, leaving 12 stitches.

Just like with the belt, you can now see the basic shape of the headscarf, and all that remains to be added are the ties and the beads.

If you are going on a beach vacation this year, don't forget to take these accessories. Everyone will want to know where you bought them!

12 **Row 22:** Now you are going to bring in another loose row, but without decreasing. So, using the size 19 (15mm) needle, knit all the stitches.

13 **Rows 23–28:** Repeat Rows 21 and 22 three more times. You should now have six stitches on your needle and 28 rows.

14 **Row 29:** With the size 8 (5mm) needle, decrease at the beginning and end of the row, leaving four stitches.

15 Bind off all the stitches and weave in the loose ends.

Braided ties

1 Cut six 16-inch (40cm) lengths of cotton yarn.

2 Take three lengths and use a crochet hook to thread them through one corner of the headscarf at the cast-on edge.

3 Braid the strands together for about 5 inches (12cm). Look back to page 17 if you need to jog your memory about braiding. Tie a knot at the end of the braid to secure it.

Make a beaded braid at each corner of the cast-on edge of the scarf.

4 Thread a bead onto the end of each strand and tie a double knot below it to keep the bead from falling off. Trim the ends of the yarn.

5 Now do the same at the other corner of the scarf and you have finished.

Making stitch patterns

This chapter teaches you a new stitch—the purl stitch. It is a bit different from the knit stitch, and when you mix the two together, you can make all kinds of new textures. Learn to purl and you'll be able to make rib, stockinette, and seed stitch. It's also time to learn other new skills, like knitting holes, making ladders, and knitting in the round.

Purl stitch

Now that you have mastered the knit stitch, you are ready to learn the purl stitch. Knit and purl stitches can be combined in a number of different ways to make a wonderful variety of patterns. Once you have mastered the purl stitch, there will be no limits to what you can create.

Using a smooth yarn, practice working rows of purl stitch until you really have the hang of it. Take as much practice as you need so that you can make the projects on the following pages look really special.

1 Cast on 10 to 20 stitches using the cable cast-on method shown on page 57.

2 Hold the needles and yarn in the same way as for making a knit stitch, but with the working end of the yarn at the front of the needles this time.

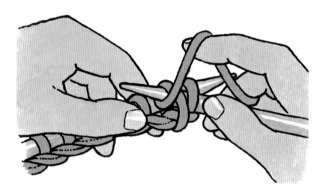

4 Using your index finger, wrap the working end of the yarn from right to left over the tip of the right needle. The yarn starts and finishes in front of the needles. If you're holding the yarn in your right hand, it will look like this.

3 Insert the right-hand needle from right to left into the front of the first stitch on the left needle so that the two needles cross each other with the right needle in front.

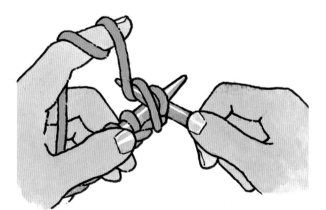

5 If you're holding the yarn in your left hand, make a stitch in exactly the same way, but use your left index finger to wrap the yarn around the right needle.

6 Lower the tip of the right needle and draw it away from you through the center of the stitch on the left needle, together with the loop of yarn. This loop will be your new stitch.

7 Pull the right needle up so that you can drop the original stitch off the left needle, keeping the new stitch on the right needle.

8 Congratulations: you have made your first purl stitch. To purl a row, repeat Steps 3–7 until all the stitches have been moved from the left needle to the right needle.

9 Now, to make another purl row, swap the needles so that the one with all the stitches is in your left hand and the empty needle is in your right hand, and start again from Step 2. Make sure that the yarn is in front of the needles before you start and remember to keep the yarn taut while you purl.

10 Continue purling each row until you have had enough practice, then bind off in the usual way.

Stitch patterns

While you are practicing, you will probably notice that the front of the purl stitch looks like the back of the knit stitch, and vice versa. See how the front of a knit stitch forms a V shape and the back forms a loop shape. Now look at how it's the front of a purl stitch that forms a loop shape and the back that forms a V shape. Different stitch patterns are made by using different combinations of these V shapes and loops. The patterns pictured here are called stockinette (above right) and reverse stockinette (below left), which you'll learn on page 73.

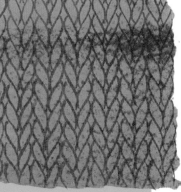

▶ **Front of knit stitch looks like back of purl stitch**

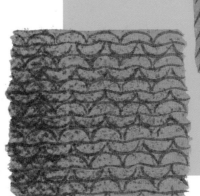

◀ **Front of purl stitch looks like back of knit stitch**

Silly sausages

This silly string of sausages gets longer and longer, as you practice different stitch patterns. Stuff them, surprise somebody, or squirt ketchup on them! So far, all the projects have been made using the knit stitch. Now it's time to learn more about the purl stitch and discover how to get textured or stretchy effects in your knitting. Making this long strip of knitting will give you a chance to practice new stitch patterns that combine the purl and the knit stitches.

This project combines knit stitch and purl stitch, so you will be using the knitting skills you learned on pages 24–31 and 70–71. You will also be using the decreasing and cable cast-on techniques on pages 56–57. If you need a reminder of how to do something, simply glance back to the pictures and instructions on those pages.

Materials

● 165 yards (150m) of worsted-weight yarn

● Size 8 (5mm) knitting needles

● Scissors

● Tapestry needle

● Stuffing

Sausage 1—single rib

This sausage uses a pattern of stitches called single rib. This is made by knitting one stitch, then purling one stitch. It creates a stretchy fabric that pulls in very narrow. It is often used for the trims on the bottom edges, cuffs, and collars of garments. The single rib pattern looks exactly the same on both sides of the knitting. Some other stitch patterns have a right side and a wrong side, so it is important to know which is the right side of your knitting when you are combining different stitch patterns.

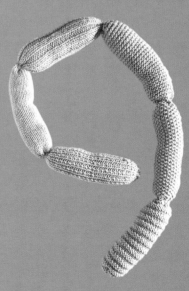

1 Cast on 28 stitches using the cable cast-on technique. When knitting single rib for the first time, it is easiest to cast on an even number of stitches, so the pattern is the same for every row.

▲ Bring the yarn to the front, ready to do a purl stitch.

2 Row 1: Knit the first stitch. Bring the yarn to the front of the knitting between the needles. Purl the next stitch.

▲ Take the yarn to the back, ready to do a knit stitch.

3 Take the yarn between the needles to the back and knit the next stitch.

4 Bring the yarn to the front again and purl the next stitch.

5 Repeat Steps 3–4, taking the yarn back to knit one stitch, then forward to purl one stitch, until you have finished the row. The last stitch will be a purl.

6 Row 2: Knit one stitch then purl one stitch to the end of the row, exactly the same as Row 1, ending with a purl stitch.

7 Repeat this row until your single ribbing is about 6 inches (15cm) long.

8 Don't bind off. You can continue to knit the next stitch pattern with the same yarn.

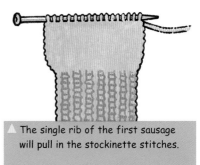

Sausage 2—stockinette stitch

This sausage uses stockinette stitch. This is the pattern of working one row of knit stitch and one row of purl stitch alternately. Stockinette is one of the most commonly used stitches because it makes a smooth, even fabric. You will see that whenever you are working a knit stitch row, the right side of the stockinette is facing you. The purl side is known as reverse stockinette. It looks a bit like garter stitch but the ridges are smaller.

▲ When you do a knit row, the right side of your knitting is facing you.

1 Row 1: When you are knitting Row 1 of stockinette stitch, the right side of your knitting will be facing you. Knit all stitches for the first row.

2 Row 2: Purl all stitches for the second row. You will see that the wrong side of your knitting is facing you now.

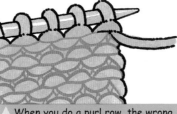

▲ When you do a purl row, the wrong side of your knitting is facing you.

3 Repeat Steps 1–2 until your stockinette is about 6 inches (15cm) long. Make sure that the last row is a purl row with the wrong side facing you.

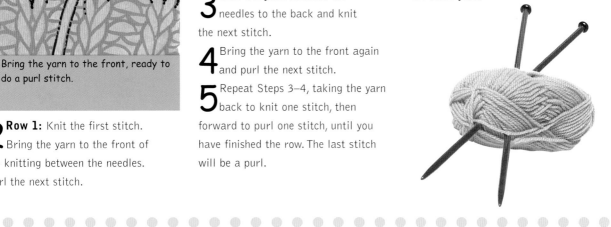

▲ The single rib of the first sausage will pull in the stockinette stitches.

4 You will notice that the single rib that you knitted first pulls in the stockinette. Don't worry. Although you have the same amount of stitches in a row, the different stitch patterns will knit up to different widths. This can be useful, especially when shaping knitted clothes.

5 Check that you still have 28 stitches on your needle and you will be ready to knit the next sausage.

Sausage 3—double rib

Knit two stitches, purl two stitches—that's how easy it is to make double rib. Double rib is stretchy, like single rib, but gives wider vertical lines of stitches. It looks the same on the right and wrong sides. It also pulls in the stockinette.

1 **Row 1:** Knit the first and second stitches. Bring the yarn to the front, just like you did in Step 2 of Sausage 1, and purl the next two stitches.

2 Repeat these four stitches along the row, remembering to take the yarn to the back before knitting two stitches and bring the yarn to the front before purling two stitches. The last two stitches will be purl.

3 **Row 2:** Repeat Row 1. You will see that you are knitting into the purl stitches of the previous row and purling into the knit stitches. This is always how you make a rib.

▲ Knit two stitches, then purl two stitches all along each row.

4 Repeat Steps 1–3 until you have about 6 inches (15cm) of double rib.

Sausage 4— garter stitch

If you purl all your rows, the knitting looks exactly the same as the garter stitch that you have been using for projects until now. It looks the same on the right and wrong sides.

1 **Row 1:** Purl all the stitches on the first row.

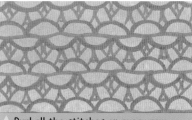

▲ Purl all the stitches on every row.

2 Continue to purl all rows until the purl knitting measures about 6 inches (15cm). You should still have 28 stitches on your needles.

Sizzling patterns!

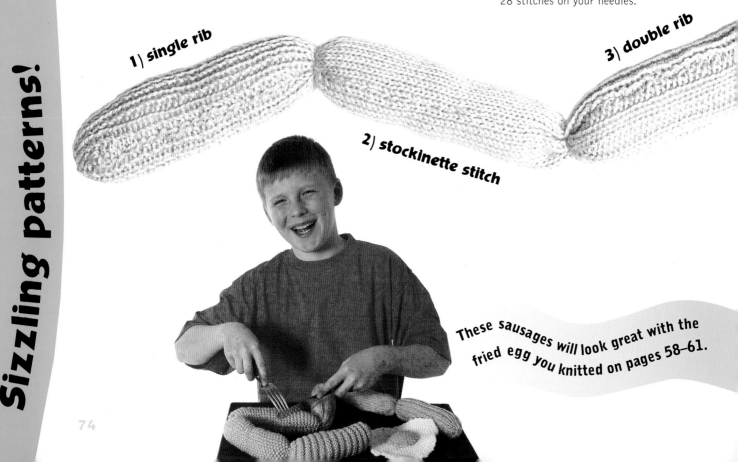

1) single rib

2) stockinette stitch

3) double rib

These sausages will look great with the fried egg you knitted on pages 58–61.

Sausage 5—seed stitch

This sausage uses seed stitch. Like single rib, but with an odd number of stitches, seed stitch makes a firm fabric that has the same bumpy texture on both sides. It doesn't curl up at the edges, so it is often used for edges and bands.

1 Seed stitch is easiest when knitted with an odd number of stitches in a row, so we need to decrease one stitch at the end of the first row, leaving 27 stitches on your needle.
Row 1: Knit into the first stitch. Bring the yarn to the front as usual and purl into the next stitch. Take the yarn to the back again. Continue to knit one stitch, purl one stitch until you reach the last two stitches. Knit two stitches together to decrease one stitch, like you did on page 56.

2 **Row 2:** Knit one, purl one to the end of the row. The last stitch will be a knit.

▲ Continue to knit one stitch, purl one stitch on every row.

3 Repeat Row 2 until your seed stitch sausage is about 6 inches (15cm) long.

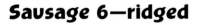

5) seed stitch

4) garter stitch

6) ridged

Sausage 6—ridged

The ridges on this sausage are simply stripes of stockinette and reverse stockinette stitch. This fabric spreads wide and shrinks up short. It is reversible, because the pattern looks the same on both sides of the fabric.

1 **Row 1:** Knit one row.
Row 2: Purl one row.
Row 3: Purl one row.
Row 4: Knit one row.

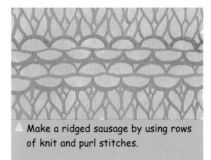

▲ Make a ridged sausage by using rows of knit and purl stitches.

2 Repeat these four rows until the ridged knitting is about 6 inches (15cm) long.

3 Bind off all the stitches. You have now completed all six sausages.

Sizzling patterns!

Backstitch seam

Backstitch makes a strong seam, and is good for lighter weight yarns. It can be a bit bulky if used with thick yarns.

1 Thread a tapestry needle with a spare length of yarn. Fold the knitting in half lengthwise, with right sides facing, making sure that the stitches are matching row for row.

2 Starting with the first row of knitting at the right-hand end, make two strong overcasting stitches to join the first stitches together and fix the end of the yarn.

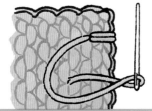

▲ Bring the needle up between Row 1 and Row 2.

3 Keeping exactly one stitch from the edge, bring the needle up through both pieces of knitting between the stitches of the first and second rows.

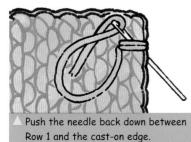

▲ Push the needle back down between Row 1 and the cast-on edge.

4 Push the needle down between the first row and the cast-on edge.

5 Bring the needle up between the second and third rows.

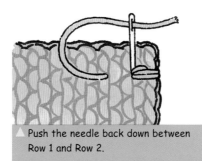

▲ Push the needle back down between Row 1 and Row 2.

6 Push the needle down between the stitches of the first and second rows, where the previous stitch started.

7 Bring the needle up two more rows, between the third and fourth rows.

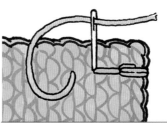

▲ Push the needle back down between Row 2 and Row 3.

8 Push the needle back down where the previous stitch started, between the second and third rows.

9 Continue in the same way to make a continuous line of stitches on the side of the knitting facing you.

▲ Secure the end of the seam with a couple of overcasting stitches.

10 When you reach the end of the side seam, use overcasting stitches to fasten the yarn end.

Stuffing the sausages

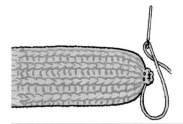

▲ Turn your knitting right side out, so that the seam stitching is hidden.

1 Now that you have a long tube, the next stage is to turn the knitting right side out. Use your fingers or the blunt end of a knitting needle to push the knitting through.

▲ Sew a running stitch around one of the open ends.

2 Thread a darning needle with more spare yarn and make a running stitch around one of the open ends to gather it up, just like you did when making the Giant Mohair Flower on page 43. Pull the yarn tight, knot securely, and trim the ends.

3 Push some stuffing right down into the tube until you have filled the first sausage. Roll the sausage between your hands to even out the stuffing.

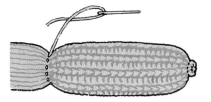

⚠ Sew a running stitch at the end of the stuffed sausage.

4 Sew a running stitch along the last row of the stuffed sausage. Pull tight, knot the yarn tightly, weave in the ends, and trim.

5 Repeat Steps 3–4 with each sausage until you complete the whole string.

You have learned lots of new stitches and made a silly string of sausages. Now it's time to swing them around and show all your friends what fun knitting can be.

Dressy clutch bag

With this sparkly purse, sprinkled with tiny holes and spangled with giant sequins, you'll be the star of the party. This bag looks great knitted in worsted-weight yarn mixed with glittery crochet thread, but you can follow the pattern with almost any yarn—just use the needles recommended on your yarn band. You will be using stockinette stitch and learning to make yarnover holes.

To make more interesting items, you need to start using all your new knitting skills together, but don't worry if that sounds daunting. Just remember to look at the pictures and instructions on pages 24–31, 54–57, and 70–71 if you need extra help with any of the techniques.

Yarnovers

A yarnover is a way of increasing an extra stitch and at the same time creating a decorative hole. Yarnovers are used when knitting lace and also for making eyelets and buttonholes. A yarnover is often used in combination with a decrease, to make a hole without adding any stitches to the row. You may want to practice making a few yarnover holes with some scrap yarn before you start the bag.

Bring the yarn to the front of your knitting.

1 Knit as far as the place where you want to make the yarnover. Bring the yarn to the front of your knitting, between the needles, as if you were about to purl a stitch.

Wrap the yarn over the top of the right needle and continue knitting.

2 Wrap the yarn over the top of the right needle and knit the next stitch. The wrapped yarn becomes a new stitch.

Purl all the stitches on the next row, including the new yarnover stitch.

3 On the next row, make sure that you purl the new stitch.

Materials

- 110 yards (100m) of worsted-weight yarn in the main color

- 30 yards (25m) of worsted-weight yarn in a contrasting color

- 110 yards (100m) of glittery crochet thread in the main color

- 30 yards (25m) of glittery crochet thread in a contrasting color

- Size 8 (5mm) knitting needles

- Scissors

- Tapestry needle

- Pins

- Button

- Size G or H (4 or 5mm) crochet hook

- Sequins

- Sewing thread and needle

Stockinette stitch

If you are confident at doing yarnovers, let's get started on the project. The bag is knitted in stockinette stitch, which you practiced when you made the Silly Sausages on page 73.

1 Hold the ends of the contrast color worsted-weight yarn and contrast color glittery crochet thread together. Make a single slip knot using both pieces of yarn. Cast on 45 stitches, using the worsted and glittery yarns together as if they were one yarn.

Make sure you work every stitch with both yarns together.

2 Work one row in knit stitch. Be careful that you always work with both yarns together throughout the project.

3 Work the second row in purl stitch, again making sure that you use both yarns.

Count the lines of Vs to check how many rows you have knitted.

4 You will remember from the Silly Sausages project that one row knit and one row purl makes stockinette stitch. Continue knitting in stockinette stitch until you have 20 rows. It is easy to count rows of stockinette stitch because each row looks like a line of Vs.

5 Now change to the main color, again mixing the worsted yarn and glittery crochet thread together. Look at page 48 of the Supersize Scarf to remind yourself how to tie in a new yarn. Work 60 rows in stockinette stitch, ending on a purl row. Do not bind off.

Just look at how the glittery crochet thread makes the purse sparkle!

Picking up dropped stockinette stitches

You learned how to pick up dropped garter stitches on page 49 of the Supersize Scarf. You will need to use a slightly different technique if you drop any stockinette stitches.

On a knit row

Keep the knit side facing you when you pick up the stitch.

1 Hold the knitting with the knit side facing you.

Insert the right needle through the dropped stitch and under the strand from front to back.

2 Insert the tip of the right-hand needle through the dropped stitch, from front to back, and then under the strand above it in the same way, from front to back.

Use the left needle to pass the picked-up stitch over the strand.

3 Use the point of the left needle to lift the picked-up stitch and pass it over the strand. Now slip the stitch off the needle, just like binding off, leaving the repaired stitch on the right needle.

Slip the repaired stitch onto the left needle.

4 Put the tip of the left needle through the repaired stitch from front to back and slip the stitch onto the left needle, ready to be worked in the usual way.

On a purl row

Keep the purl side facing you when you pick up the stitch.

1 Hold the piece of knitting with the purl side facing you.

Insert the right needle through the dropped stitch and under the strand from back to front.

2 Insert the tip of the right needle through the dropped stitch, from back to front, and then insert the tip of the needle under the strand above it the same way, from back to front.

Use the left needle to pass the picked-up stitch over the strand.

3 Use the point of the left needle to lift the picked-up stitch and pass it over the strand. Now slip the stitch off the needle, just like binding off, leaving the repaired stitch on the right needle.

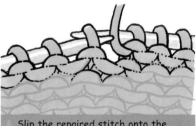

Slip the repaired stitch onto the left needle.

4 Put the tip of the left needle through the repaired stitch from front to back and slip the stitch onto the left needle, ready to be worked in the usual way.

Lace pattern

To make the lace-hole patterned flap of the bag, we will be using the knit 2 together decrease, then making a yarnover.

1 This is the first lace pattern row. **Row 81:** *Knit four stitches, then knit the next two stitches together. Now bring the yarn forward to make a yarnover.* Repeat the pattern between the asterisks six more times, then knit the last three stitches.

2 **Row 82:** Purl all stitches, making sure that you purl into all the yarnover loops and still have 45 stitches at the end of the row.

3 **Row 83:** Knit all stitches.
Row 84: Purl all stitches.

4 This is the second lace pattern row. **Row 85:** Knit two stitches, then knit the next two stitches together. Bring the yarn forward to make a yarnover. *Knit four stitches, then knit the next two stitches together. Now bring the yarn forward to make a yarnover.* Repeat the pattern between the asterisks five more times, then knit the last five stitches.

5 **Row 86:** Purl all stitches.
Row 87: Knit all stitches.
Row 88: Purl all stitches.

6 This is the third lace pattern row. **Row 89:** *Knit four stitches, then knit the next two stitches together. Now bring the yarn forward to make a yarnover.* Repeat the pattern between the asterisks six more times, then knit the last three stitches.

7 **Row 90:** Purl all stitches.
Row 91: Knit all stitches.
Row 92: Purl all stitches.

8 This is the fourth lace pattern row. **Row 93:** Knit the first six stitches, then knit the next two stitches together.

Asterisks

As you work through this project, you will often come across a pair of asterisks (small stars) surrounding a set of instructions within the pattern. This saves on having to spell out the whole sequence again when it needs repeating. Instead, the pattern will tell you to repeat the stitches between the asterisks. For example: *Knit two stitches, purl two stitches.* Repeat two more times. This means knit two, purl two, knit two, purl two, knit two, purl two. Just imagine how much space it would take if you had to write out the sequence 20 times!

Bring the yarn forward to make a yarnover. *Knit four stitches, then knit the next two stitches together. Now bring the yarn forward to make a yarnover.* Repeat the pattern between the asterisks five more times, then knit the last stitch.

9 **Row 94:** Purl all stitches.
Row 95: Knit all stitches.
Row 96: Purl all stitches.

10 This is the fifth lace pattern row. **Row 97:** Knit the first eight stitches, then knit the next two stitches together. Bring the yarn forward to make a yarnover. *Knit four stitches, then knit the next two stitches together. Now bring the yarn forward to make a yarnover.* Repeat the pattern between the asterisks four more times, then knit the last five stitches.

11 **Row 98:** Purl all stitches.
Row 99: Knit all stitches.

Seed stitch trim

1 Check that you still have an odd number of stitches on your needle— you should have 45 in total.
Rows 100–102: *Knit one stitch. Purl one stitch.* Repeat along the row, ending with a knit stitch.

2 Bind off all the stitches, weave in the loose ends, and trim.

Phew! Now that the main part and the flap are done, let's start adding the trimmings and sewing it up.

Sewing the seams and button

1 Fold the bag right sides together so that the cast-on edge nearly reaches the first lace-hole row. Use a few pins to hold it in place.

Backstitch the side seams.

2 With a tapestry needle and the main color of worsted-weight yarn, backstitch both side seams securely, like you did on page 76 of the Silly Sausages project.

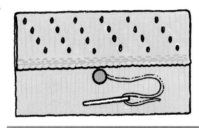

Sew a button to the front of the bag in the center.

3 Turn the bag right side out. Use the same yarn to stitch a button in the center of the front of the bag, so that it sits just below the flap.

Crocheting the loop

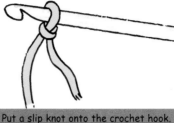

Put a slip knot onto the crochet hook.

1 You now need to use a crochet hook to make a chain loop for fastening the button. Crochet is just like finger knitting, but finer. Make a slip knot with the main worsted-weight yarn and put it onto the crochet hook.

Push the hook through a stitch at the edge of the flap in the center.

2 Push the tip of the hook through a stitch at the center of the last row of knitting on the flap.

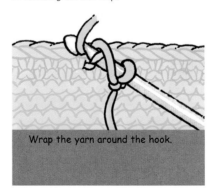

Wrap the yarn around the hook.

3 Wrap the yarn around the tip of the crochet hook.

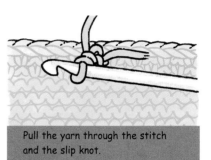

Pull the yarn through the stitch and the slip knot.

4 Use the hook to pull the yarn through the stitch and the slip knot, making a loop on the crochet hook. This is the first stitch.

5 Wrap the yarn around the tip of the hook and pull it through the first stitch. This is the second stitch.

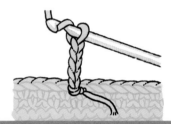

Make a chain of stitches to fit around the button.

6 Repeat Step 5 to continue making a chain of stitches until it is long enough to go around the button.

7 Cut the thread, leaving a 6-inch (15cm) tail of yarn.

8 Use the hook to pull the end of the yarn right through the last stitch and pull to tighten.

Sew the end of the chain to the flap to make a loop.

9 Thread the tapestry needle with the end of the yarn and stitch securely into place on the wrong side of the bag flap, just next to the beginning of the chain, making a loop.

10 Weave in the ends and hook the loop over the button to fasten your bag.

Now all you need to do is sew some sequins onto the bag for even more sparkle. Look back to page 44 to remind yourself how to do this.

Floppy dollies

Make a cute and cuddly doll with floppy arms and legs, or swap the braided hair for pointy ears and, presto, you have a bunny! These dolls use simple shaping techniques in stockinette stitch, and when they are finished, you can knit miniature clothes with scraps of yarn.

To make these dolls, you need to use nearly all the knitting skills you have learned so far. From now on, we will no longer tell you which increase or decrease method to use, just like in real knitting patterns. So, if you forget anything, look back at the pictures and instructions on pages 24–31, 54–57, and 70–71 for a bit of extra guidance.

Floppy doll

Front

Start your floppy doll by knitting the front piece, working from the legs up to the head.

Knitting the first leg

1 Cast on eight stitches in the shoe yarn on size 6 (4mm) needles.

2 Row 1: Knit one row.
Row 2: Purl one row.

3 Row 3: Knit one row, increasing one stitch at the beginning and one stitch at the end of the row.

4 Rows 4–9: Repeat Rows 2 and 3 three more times, until you have 16 stitches and nine rows on your needle.
Row 10: Purl one row.

5 Change to the body yarn and work in stockinette stitch to Row 50. Look at page 48 of the Supersize Scarf to remind yourself of how to tie in a new yarn.

6 Trim the yarn, leaving a 6-inch (15cm) tail. You now need to put the stitches onto a stitch holder or large safety pin while you knit the other leg.

Knitting the second leg

1 Cast on eight stitches in the shoe yarn and work exactly as you did for the first leg as far as Row 50. Don't forget to change color on Row 11.

2 Row 51: Knit across the 16 stitches and then cast on two stitches. Put the needle to one side for a moment.

3 You now need to put the stitches from the stitch holder back onto the empty size 6 (4mm) knitting needle. When all the stitches are on the needle, put the needle in your left hand, and put down the stitch holder.

Body

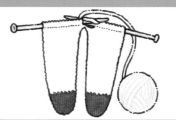

Knit across the stitches you picked up from the stitch holder to join the legs together.

1 Row 1: Pick up the other needle (the one holding the second leg) in your right hand and knit across the stitches that you have just picked up from the stitch holder. Pull the yarn tightly as you knit into the first stitch so that you get a neat join. Both legs are now hanging from the same needle and you have 34 stitches on the needle.

2 Row 2: Purl all stitches.
Rows 3–18: Starting with a knit row, continue working all stitches in stockinette stitch for 16 more rows.

Using a stitch holder

When knitting some patterns, you will need to leave stitches on a stitch holder to be worked into at a later stage. A stitch holder looks like a large safety pin with a blunt point.

1 To put stitches onto a stitch holder, hold the needle with the stitches in your left hand. Insert the tip of the stitch holder into the first stitch.

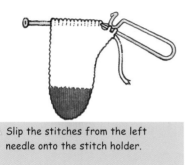

⚠ Slip the stitches from the left needle onto the stitch holder.

2 Slip the stitch from the left needle onto the holder. Work along the row of stitches, one by one, in the same way. When the required number of stitches are on the holder, close it and put it safely aside.

3 To pick up stitches from a stitch holder when you need to use them again, hold the stitch holder in your left hand. Hold the empty needle in your right hand and insert the needle into the first stitch on the stitch holder.

4 Slip the stitch from the holder onto the right needle. Work along the row of stitches, one by one, in the same way. When the required number of stitches are on the needle, put the needle in your left hand, and put down the stitch holder.

Materials

● 200 yards (180m) of worsted-weight yarn for the body

● 11 yards (10m) of worsted-weight yarn for the shoes

● 30 yards (25m) of worsted-weight yarn for the hair

● 70 yards (60m) of worsted-weight yarn in various colors for the dress

● Size 6 (4mm) knitting needles

● Size 8 (5mm) knitting needles

● Stitch holder or large safety pin

● Scissors

● Tapestry needle

● 2 toy eyes or buttons plus 2 buttons for the dress

● Scraps of yarn for embroidery

● Pins

● Stuffing

● Crochet hook

3 **Row 19:** You are now going to shape the shoulders. Knit one row, decreasing one stitch at the beginning and one stitch at the end of the row.
Row 20: Purl one row.
4 **Rows 21–40:** Repeat Rows 19 and 20 for 20 more rows. When you have finished, you will have 12 stitches on your needle.

Neck and head shaping

1 **Rows 1–4:** Work four rows in stockinette stitch.
2 **Rows 5–10:** For the next six rows of stockinette, increase one stitch at the beginning and one stitch at the end of each row. You will have 24 stitches on your needle.
3 **Rows 11–22:** Work 12 rows of stockinette stitch with no shaping.

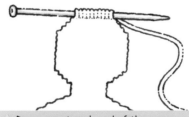

⚠ Decrease at each end of the rows to shape the top of the head.

4 **Rows 23–30:** For the next eight rows of stockinette, decrease one stitch at the beginning and one stitch at the end of each row. You will have eight stitches left on your needle.

5 **Row 31:** Knit one row and bind off all the stitches.

Back

Follow all the steps in the Front section to knit the back exactly the same as the front.

Arms

You need to make two arms in exactly the same way, working in stockinette stitch and starting with the hands.

Shaping the hands

1 Cast on ten stitches in the body yarn on size 6 (4mm) knitting needles.

2 **Row 1:** Knit one row.
Row 2: Purl one row.

3 **Row 3:** Knit one row, increasing one stitch at the beginning and one stitch at the end of the row.
Row 4: Purl one row.

4 **Rows 5–12:** Repeat Rows 3 and 4 four more times, giving you 20 stitches and 12 rows.

5 **Row 13:** Knit one row.
Row 14: Purl one row, decreasing one stitch at the beginning and one stitch at the end of the row.

6 **Row 15:** Knit one row, decreasing one stitch at the beginning and one stitch at the end of the row, leaving 16 stitches.

7 **Row 16:** Purl one row.
Row 17: Knit one row.
Row 18: Purl one row.

Shaping the arm

1 **Rows 19–22:** Increase one stitch at the beginning and end of each row for the next four rows of stockinette stitch. You will have 24 stitches and 22 rows.

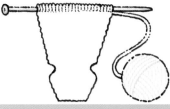

⚠ Use stockinette stitch to lengthen the shaped arm.

2 **Rows 23–44:** Work another 22 rows of stockinette stitch to Row 44. Do not increase or decrease on these rows.

3 Bind off all the stitches. Remember to knit a second arm in exactly the same way.

Assembling the doll

Adding the face

Sew on some toy eyes or buttons and a smiley mouth, like you did for the Funny-face Bag on pages 32–33, using a tapestry needle and scraps of yarn.

Sewing and stuffing

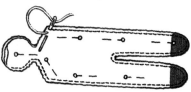

⚠ Sew the front and back together, leaving the top of the head open.

1 Put the back and front together, right sides facing, and use pins to hold the pieces in position. Using a tapestry needle and the main body yarn,

backstitch the pieces together around the edge, like you did on page 76 of the Silly Sausages project. Leave the bind-off edges at the top of the head open. Remove the pins.

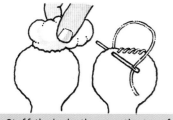

⚠ Stuff the body, then sew the top of the head closed.

2 Turn the doll right side out, then fill the body with stuffing. Use a knitting needle to push it right down the legs. Use a small version of the overcast stitch that you learned on page 34 to close the opening at the top of the head.

3 Fold one arm in half lengthwise, right sides facing, and backstitch the side seam with the main yarn, leaving the top open. Turn right side out. Repeat with the other arm.

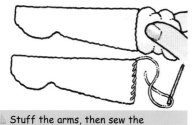

⚠ Stuff the arms, then sew the tops closed.

4 Fill the arms with stuffing and use a small overcast stitch to close them up.

⚠ Sew the arms to the body.

5 Sew the arms securely in place on the body using overcast stitches.

Making the hair

1 Cut lots of strands of the hair yarn, each about 10 inches (25cm) long.

⚠ Use a crochet hook to pull a bunch of hair through the top of the head.

2 Take a bunch of five or six strands and use a crochet hook to pull one end of the strands through the knitting at the top of the head.

⚠ Tie a knot next to the head to hold the hair in place.

3 Pull the yarn through until both ends are even, then tie in a knot next to the head to hold it in place.

4 Repeat Steps 2–3 five mores times, so that you have six bunches of hair across the top of the head.

⚠ Make two braids and tie the ends with colorful yarn.

5 Braid three bunches of hair on one side of the head, then braid the remaining three bunches of hair on the other side of the head. If you need any help, look back at the braiding technique on page 17. Tie the ends of the two braids with a length of yarn in a contrasting color.

Wow! Isn't it great to be able to knit your own toys? Now that your floppy doll is complete, you can decide on her name while you knit her a little dress.

Project 11

Knitting a dress

The doll's dress is knitted in stripes of different colored yarns. You can use any stripe pattern that you like.

Knitting the stripes

1 On size 8 (5mm) knitting needles, cast on 68 stitches in the dress yarn and work four rows in knit stitch.

2 Using a size 6 (4mm) needle, purl one row.

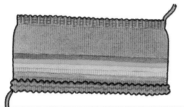

Knit stripes of color on the dress.

3 Now bring in the other size 6 (4mm) needle and begin knitting stockinette stitch, changing color whenever you like. Look at page 48 of the Supersize Scarf to remind yourself of how to tie in a new yarn. Knit 22 rows of stockinette stitch.

4 Now work four rows in single rib (knit one stitch, purl one stitch). Bind off.

Knitting the straps

1 Cast on five stitches on size 6 (4mm) needles and knit 70 rows in garter stitch (knit all stitches).

2 Bind off and make another strap in the same way.

Assembling the dress

1 Backstitch the back seam, as you did for the doll.

2 Put the dress onto the doll and pin the straps into place. They should cross over each other and tuck inside the dress at the back, and sit on the outside of the dress at the front.

Sew the crossed-over straps inside the back of the dress.

3 Slip the dress off the doll and use a tapestry needle and a scrap of yarn to stitch the straps into place at the back of the dress.

Sew a button onto each strap at the front of the dress.

4 Place a button on each strap where it overlaps the dress at the front and sew the button into place through the strap and the dress.

Now put the dress back on the doll and admire your handiwork. If you are feeling up to the challenge, why not make the bunny as well?

Floppy bunny

Materials

- 220 yards (200m) of worsted-weight yarn for the body and outside ears
- 25 yards (20m) of worsted-weight yarn for the paws and inside ears
- 35 yards (30m) of worsted-weight yarn for the tail
- 15 yards (10m) of orange worsted-weight yarn for the carrot tie
- Size 6 (4mm) knitting needles
- Stitch holder or large safety pin
- Scissors
- 2 toy eyes or buttons
- Tapestry needle
- Scraps of yarn for embroidery, including green
- Pins
- Stuffing
- Two 2-inch (5cm) diameter cardboard disks with 1-inch (2.5cm) diameter holes for pompom making
- 4 inches (10cm) of narrow elastic

Body and arms

Knit the front of the body in exactly the same way as you knit the floppy doll, but knit the legs in the main color only because bunnies don't wear shoes! Knit the back in the same way as the doll, starting with the paw color for the first ten rows of the legs. Knit the arms just like you did for the doll.

Floppy ears

You need to make two ears alike. Remember to knit the outside and inside ears in different colors.

Outside ear

1 Cast on 18 stitches using the body color yarn.

2 **Row 1:** Knit all stitches.
Row 2: Purl all stitches.

3 **Row 3:** Knit one row, increasing one stitch at the beginning and one stitch at the end of the row.
Row 4: Purl all stitches.

4 **Rows 5–10:** Repeat Rows 3 and 4 three more times, giving you 26 stitches on your needle.

5 **Rows 11–22:** Work 12 rows in stockinette stitch, giving you 22 rows.

6 **Row 23:** Knit one row, decreasing one stitch at the beginning and one stitch at the end of the row.
Row 24: Purl all stitches.

7 **Rows 25–44:** Repeat Rows 23 and 24 ten more times. When you have finished, you will have four stitches left on the needle.

8 Bind off. Remember to make a second outside ear in exactly the same way.

Inside ear

1 Cast on eight stitches using the inside ears yarn.

2 Work 30 rows in stockinette stitch (one row knit, one row purl).

3 **Row 31:** Knit one row, decreasing one stitch at the beginning and one stitch at the end of the row.
Row 32: Purl all stitches.

4 Repeat Rows 31 and 32 until you have only one stitch left.

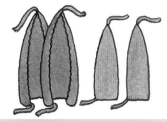

Make two outside ears and two inside ears.

5 Bind off the last stitch. Remember to make a second inside ear in exactly the same way so that you have two outside and two inside pieces.

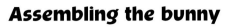

Assembling the bunny

Follow the instructions for Assembling the Doll. Don't add the hair, of course; the bunny needs ears and a tail instead.

Adding the face

1 Use a tapestry needle and a scrap of yarn to sew some toy eyes or buttons on the front of the head. (The front is the piece of knitting without the paws.)

Sew the mouth just below the eyes in the center of the face.

2 Sew a big X for the mouth and do a little stitch over the center to hold it in place.

Adding the ears

1 Pin the inside ear piece flat onto the main ear with wrong sides facing and the cast-on edges touching.

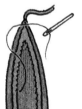

Stitch the inside ear piece onto the center of the outside ear piece.

2 Using the main body yarn and the tapestry needle, stitch the two pieces together around the edges of the inside ear piece. The edges of the outside ear piece will roll around to make a good shape.

Sew the tips of the ears into a pointy shape.

3 Sew the edges at the tips of the outside ear piece together to make them pointed.

Sew the bottom edges together to make the ears curvy.

4 Fold the bottom edges of the ear inward until they touch each other, and stitch into place.

Stitch the ears to the top of the head.

5 Pin the ears into place on the head and stitch securely, like you sewed the arms.

Adding the tail

Make a pompom following the instructions on page 16, but don't trim the tied ends of yarn. Thread the ends onto a tapestry needle and use them to stitch the tail securely into place on the bunny's bottom.

Carrot tie

A carrot tie is all that is needed to dress up the rabbit. The tie is knitted in garter stitch, where all rows are knit stitch.

Knitting the tie

1 Cast on three stitches in orange yarn. Knit one row.

2 Increase one stitch at the beginning of the next eight rows until you have 11 stitches.

3 Knit eight rows without increasing any more stitches.

4 Decrease one stitch at both ends of the next row so that you have nine stitches.

5 Knit three rows without decreasing any more stitches.

6 Decrease one stitch at both ends of the next row.

7 Knit nine rows of seven stitches. Bind off.

Making the knot for the tie

1 Cast on six stitches. Work 16 rows in knit stitch. Bind off.

Assembling the tie

Stitch the knot to the tie with small, neat stitches.

1 Fold the knot in half and stitch it to the top of the tie.

⚠ Attach some elastic to the back of the knot big enough to fit over the bunny's head.

2 Thread a piece of elastic through the back of the knot on the tie. Tie the ends of the elastic together, then check that it will fit over the bunny's head. Undo the knot and try again if it doesn't. When the knot's in the right place, trim the ends of the elastic.

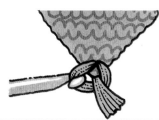

⚠ Make a green leafy tassel at the tip of the tie.

3 Cut a few short pieces of green yarn and pull them through the tip of the tie with a crochet hook to make a leafy tassel.

The doll and bunny make a great pair. Perhaps you could knit them to give as a present to a younger sister, brother, cousin, or friend.

Plaid poncho

This poncho will dazzle everybody with its color and pattern. It is knitted in horizontally striped stockinette stitch with no shaping. To create the plaid effect, just drop some stitches on the last row of knitting and watch them run! Then weave contrast colors through the ladders to create the vertical lines. Finish off with fringe. The poncho measures 18 inches (45cm) from neck to wrist, before the fringe is added.

Remind yourself of the skills needed to knit this poncho by looking at pages 24–31, 57, and 70–71.

Measuring gauge

When knitting items of clothing, it's important for your piece of knitting to end up the right size so that it fits you. To check that the size will be okay, you need to knit a test piece about 5 x 5 inches (12 x 12cm), following the instructions of the main knitting pattern and using the recommended needle size. You then count the number of stitches and rows in the test piece. This is called measuring the gauge. All knitting patterns tell you how many stitches and rows you should have across a certain measurement.

1 To knit a test piece for the poncho, cast on 30 stitches and follow the pattern instructions for Steps 1–3 of Knitting the Poncho Front, until it measures about 5 inches (12cm) long.

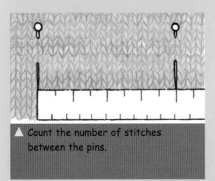

▲ Count the number of stitches between the pins.

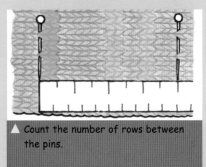

▲ Count the number of rows between the pins.

2 Lay a ruler across the width of the test piece. Push a pin through the knitting at the beginning of the ruler and then push another pin into the knitting 4 inches (10cm) across. Remove the ruler and count how many stitches (V shapes) there are between the two pins. Write the number down and remove the pins.

3 Measure 4 inches (10cm) down the length of the test piece, using pins to mark the knitting like you did in Step 2. Remove the ruler and count how many rows there are between the pins. An easy way to count rows is to

count from the point of one V shape to the point of the next. Write the number down and remove the pins.

4 The gauge for this poncho is 22 stitches to 4 inches (10cm) and 28 rows to 4 inches (10cm). If your test piece has more stitches and rows than this, you will need to use larger needles than the pattern says. If your test piece has fewer stitches and rows than this, you will need to use smaller needles than the pattern says.

5 Knit another test piece with the new size needles and measure it like before. Keep trying until you get the right size.

Materials

- 765 yards (700m) of worsted-weight yarn in the main color A

- 275 yards (250m) of worsted-weight yarn in the contrast color B

- 165 yards (150m) of worsted-weight yarn in the contrast color C

- 165 yards (150m) of worsted-weight yarn for the fringe

- Size 6 (4mm) knitting needles

- Size 4 (3.5mm) knitting needles

- Pencil and paper

- Scissors

- Tapestry needle

- 2 large towels

- Pins

- Tape measure

- Crochet hook

Keep a pencil and paper handy so that you can make a note of where you are on the stripe pattern while you knit so that you don't get confused.

Front

Knitting the poncho

1 Cast on 86 stitches in the main yarn A on size 6 (4mm) knitting needles. Remember to use bigger or smaller needles if you need to, depending on your gauge test piece. Work in stockinette stitch (knit one row, purl one row) for eight rows.

2 Change to contrast yarn B. The poncho is knitted in stripes, so you will be changing color quite often. Look at page 48 of the Supersize Scarf to remind yourself of how to tie in a new yarn.

3 From now on, you will be following the stripe pattern and continuing in stockinette stitch. Work the stripes as follows:

*Two rows B
Two rows A
Two rows B
Six rows A
Two rows C
Six rows A
Two rows B
Two rows A
Two rows B
Fourteen rows A*

4 You now have 48 rows. Repeat the pattern in Step 3, between the asterisks, three more times. You now have 168 rows, and I bet you're glad you had that pencil and paper.

5 Continue in stockinette stitch and work the next stripes as follows:

Two rows B
Two rows A
Two rows B
Six rows A
Two rows C
Six rows A
Two rows B
Two rows A
Two rows B
Eight rows A

Well done! You have finished knitting the first half of the poncho. Now it's time to make the ladders that will become the vertical stripes.

Making the ladders

1 Get a pencil and some paper ready, because you will need to keep count when making the ladders. Working with yarn A, bind off the first 15 stitches as usual. You will have one stitch on the right needle.

▲ Drop the next stitch off the end of the left needle.

2 Slide the next stitch off the end of the left needle and drop it!

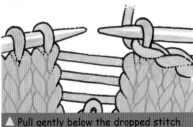

▲ Pull gently below the dropped stitch to see it unravel down the knitting.

3 If you pull gently below the dropped stitch, it will undo and start to run down your knitting. However, do this only on the first dropped stitch, just to see what happens. Leave the next dropped stitches alone while you are binding off. You will unravel them later.

▲ Bind off three more stitches, including the stitch on your right needle from Step 1.

4 Bind off three more stitches. Don't forget to bind off the stitch that was on your right needle in Step 1. You will have a new single stitch on your right needle when you have finished.

5 Drop the next stitch as in Step 2, but don't unravel it.

6 Bind off five stitches and drop the next stitch.

7 Bind off five stitches and drop the next stitch.

8 Now bind off three stitches and drop the next stitch.

9 This time, bind off 14 stitches and drop the next stitch.

10 Now repeat the binding off and drop-stitch pattern from the beginning of Step 4 to the end of Step 8.

11 Bind off 14 stitches, then bind off the last stitch and secure.

12 Now you can have fun unraveling the dropped stitches to create ladders that will travel all the way down the length of the knitting. Just pull gently below the dropped stitches and they will come undone.

Mending a stockinette stitch ladder

In this project you're making ladders on purpose, but it's a good idea to learn how to mend one in case you drop a stitch and get a ladder by accident.

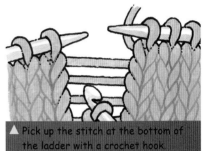

▲ Pick up the stitch at the bottom of the ladder with a crochet hook.

1 With the knit side of the fabric facing you, push a crochet hook up through the loop of the stitch at the bottom of the ladder.

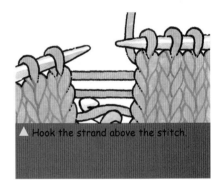

▲ Hook the strand above the stitch.

2 With the hook pointing upward, catch the first strand of the ladder.

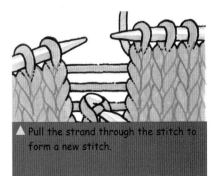

▲ Pull the strand through the stitch to form a new stitch.

3 Pull the strand through the stitch on the hook. The strand has now become a new stitch.

Try mending one of the ladders on the poncho to practice the technique—then you can have all the fun of making the ladder once again!

Check this out!

4 Repeat Steps 2–3 until all the strands have been made into new stitches.

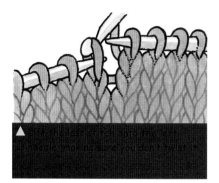

5 Lift the last stitch onto the left needle, making sure that it doesn't get twisted, and continue to work the row.

Back

Make the back half of the poncho in exactly the same way, following all the steps in the Front section.

Assembling the poncho

When you have finished the front and back, and unraveled all the ladders, you are ready to join the pieces together and add the colorful stripes and fringe.

Blocking

You will find that, because the poncho is knitted in stockinette stitch, the pieces curl up at the edges. This can make it difficult to sew. Blocking is the process of making knitted pieces stay the right shape and size.

1 Lay a large towel on a flat surface, such as a table.

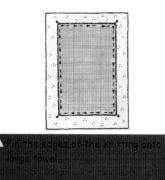
▲ Pin the edges of the knitting onto a large towel.

2 Lay one piece of knitting on the towel with the right side facing down, and pin it to the towel so that it measures the right size, keeping the edges straight. The finished measurement should be about 18 inches (45cm) wide and 28 inches (70cm) long.

3 If yours is a bit different, don't worry, but the length measurement minus the width measurement should be about 10 inches (25cm). This size allows the poncho to fit over your head easily. Knitting is quite stretchy, so be sure to make a note of your final measurements so that you can block both pieces to the same size.

4 Dampen the second towel and lay it over the knitting, making sure that the edges are covered. Pat the towel down gently to make sure that it dampens the knitting. Leave until the towel and knitting are completely dry.

5 Lift up the top towel, then take the pins out of your knitting. You will see that your knitting is now blocked to shape. Repeat with the other piece of the poncho. You can start the next stage on the first piece while you are waiting for the second piece to dry.

Threading the vertical stripes

1 Cut two 2¾-foot (80cm) lengths of yarn C and thread them both through a tapestry needle.

2 Starting with the first ladder, thread the yarn under two strands and then over two strands, all the way up the ladder.

3 Pull the yarn a little way past the end of the knitting and remove the needle. Make sure that the thread does not bunch up the knitting.

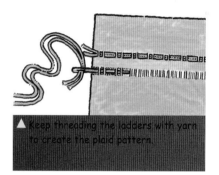
▲ Keep threading the ladders with yarn to create the plaid pattern.

4 Now follow this pattern:
Thread the second ladder in yarn C
Third ladder in yarn B
Fourth ladder in yarn C
Fifth ladder in yarn C

5 Repeat the same pattern on the next five ladders: C, C, B, C, and C.

You now have a plaid pattern on your knitting. Don't forget to repeat it on the other half of the poncho.

Project 12

Sewing up the seams

1 Place the narrow side of the first piece of the poncho along the long side of the second piece, right sides together. Make sure the corners meet. You will have made an L shape.

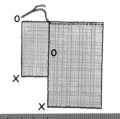

▲ Backstitch the seam.

2 Use yarn A to backstitch the seam, like you did on page 76 of the Silly Sausages project. Start by sewing along the narrow edge, overcasting to secure the ends.

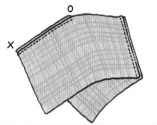

▲ Sew the two pieces together between the X and O.

3 Now bring the two corners marked X on the diagram together and pin. Bring the two points marked O together and pin. Sew both pieces together along the seam between X and O. Overcast the ends.

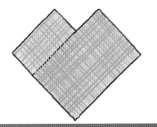

▲ Turn the poncho right side out. See how it has a V shape for the neck.

4 Turn the poncho right side out and fold it so that you have a V shape at the front and back. Using the tapestry needle, weave in all the loose strands of yarn at the neck edge, inside the seams, and at the bottom edges.

Making the neckband

1 Hold the knitting with the right side facing you. Starting at the point of a V, push a size 4 (3.5mm) knitting needle through the center of the first stitch, from front to back.

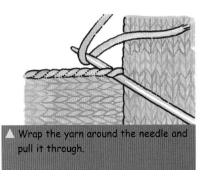

▲ Wrap the yarn around the needle and pull it through.

2 Using yarn A, wrap the yarn around the needle and pull the loop through, just like knitting a plain knit stitch.

3 Knit into the next stitch to the left along the edge of the V in the same way.

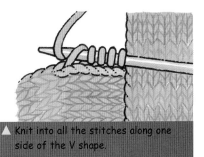

▲ Knit into all the stitches along one side of the V shape.

4 Continue to knit into the edge of the poncho, working from right to left away from the V until you reach the next point of a V.

5 Now pick up the other size 4 (3.5mm) needle and work in single rib (knit one stitch, purl one stitch) for six rows. Bind off.

6 Repeat on the other side of the V shape, picking up the same number of stitches.

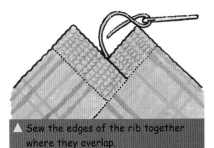

▲ Sew the edges of the rib together where they overlap.

7 Stitch the overlapping edges of the rib neatly together.

Check this out!

Fringe

Add some fringe around the bottom of the poncho, just like you did for the Funny-face Bag on page 34. Cut lots of 1-foot (30cm) lengths of yarn and use six strands at a time, using a crochet hook to add a tassel of fringe every 2 inches (5cm) all around the edge.

Any worsted-weight yarns will work for this poncho. Try using a fluffy yarn for the stripes and fringe to create a more unusual effect.

Peruvian pompom hat

For this colorful hat, you're going to use different colored yarns in stripes to create your own design. Try varying the widths of the stripes from one row to about six. The fun part of making this hat is that you get to work on circular and double-pointed needles. This is called "knitting in the round." You can also practice seed stitch, blanket stitch, and best of all, you can top it off with big rainbow-colored pompoms!

Remind yourself of the skills needed to knit this hat by looking at pages 16–17, 24–31, 54–57, and 70–71.

Super circles!

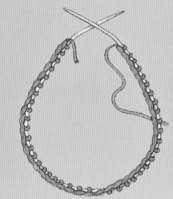

▲ Cast 96 stitches onto the circular needle.

1 Cast 96 stitches onto the circular needle. Slip a stitch marker onto the needle after you have cast on the last stitch.

2 Round 1: Purl into the first cast-on stitch so that your knitting forms a round circle. Continue to purl into each stitch until you reach the stitch marker—you have now knitted a round. Slip the stitch marker onto the other needle. Make a note on some

Making the hat

paper each time you finish a round (as you reach the marker) so that you know how many rounds you have knitted.

3 Rounds 2–4: Purl three more rounds. You have now knitted four rounds. Look at the knitting—you'll see that you are knitting reverse stockinette stitch.

4 Change color for the next stripe. Keep changing color every so often—wherever you like—to create more stripes.

5 Rounds 5–24: Knit for 20 more rounds. You will now use knit stitch for the rest of the knitting, but amazingly, you'll see that knitting in rounds gives stockinette stitch.

6 Round 25: This is where you begin to decrease. Knit 22 stitches, then knit two stitches together, and put a second color stitch marker onto the needle. Repeat this step until you reach your original stitch marker.

7 You have now decreased a total of four stitches, so you should have 92 stitches on your needle.

8 Round 26: Knit the next round without decreasing, slipping the stitch markers onto the next needle as you come to them.

9 Round 27: Now knit 21 stitches. You will see that there are two stitches left before you reach the marker—knit these two together and then slip the marker onto the next needle. Repeat this whole step three more times. You now have 88 stitches on your needle.

10 Round 28: Knit this round without decreasing, slipping the stitch markers to the next needle as you come to them.

Materials

- 265 yards (240m) of worsted-weight yarn in assorted colors

- - - - - - - - - - - - - -

- Size 6 (4mm) circular needle of 2 feet (60cm) in length

- - - - - - - - - - - - - -

- Four size 6 (4mm) double-pointed needles

- - - - - - - - - - - - - -

- Two size 6 (4mm) single-pointed needles

- - - - - - - - - - - - - -

- Pencil and paper

- - - - - - - - - - - - - -

- Cardboard disks for pompom making

- - - - - - - - - - - - - -

- Tapestry needle

Making a stitch marker

A stitch marker will help you see when you have finished a round of knitting or need to decrease. You can buy stitch markers or make your own. To make one, cut 2 inches (5cm) of yarn in a color that you will not be using in your knitting. Tie it into a loop around your needle, making sure that it doesn't grip too tightly. When you reach the stitch marker in your knitting, do not knit into it but just slip it onto the next needle and continue to knit the next stitch.

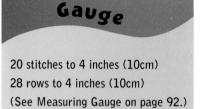

Gauge

20 stitches to 4 inches (10cm)
28 rows to 4 inches (10cm)
(See Measuring Gauge on page 92.)

11 Round 29: For this round, you need to knit 20 stitches. You will see that there are two stitches left before you reach the marker. Knit these two stitches together. Slip the stitch marker onto the next needle. Repeat this whole step three more times. You now have 84 stitches on your needle.

12 Keep knitting your work in rounds, decreasing on every other round, each time knitting one stitch less in between decreasing. Just remember to knit together the last two stitches before each marker and you won't need to count stitches.

13 You've probably noticed that as you've decreased the stitches, the knitting won't reach properly around the circular needle any more. So now you need to transfer the knitting onto double-pointed needles. To do this, knit with the first double-pointed needle into the next stitch on the circular needle.

Continue to knit until about a third of your stitches are on the new needle. Make sure the stitches are not too close to the tips of the needle.

14 Take a second double-pointed needle and continue to work around the knitting until the next third of the stitches are on this needle. Knit the remaining stitches onto a third double-pointed needle.

15 Now you can keep knitting on your double-pointed needles using the fourth (empty) needle. Continue knitting until you have finished Round 55. You should have 32 stitches.

16 Round 56: From now on you need to decrease EVERY round as follows: Starting with Round 56, knit six stitches, knit two stitches together, and slip the stitch marker. Repeat this step three more times.

17 Round 57: Knit five stitches, knit two stitches together, and slip the stitch marker. Repeat this step three more times.

18 Round 58: Knit four stitches, knit two stitches together, and slip the stitch marker. Repeat this step three more times.

19 Round 59: Knit three stitches, knit two stitches together, and slip the stitch marker. Repeat this step three more times. You now have 16 stitches.

20 During this step, remove the stitch markers as you come to them. For Round 60 to the end: knit two stitches, knit two stitches together, and then keep doing this until you have only four stitches left.

21 Put all the stitches onto one needle and knit them all together, pulling the end of the yarn through the stitches.

Earflaps

Find the beginning of your first round of knitting. This will be the center back of your hat. Select the same color yarn as you've got here to start the earflaps. You need to cast on by knitting into the cast-on edge of the hat.

Right-hand flap

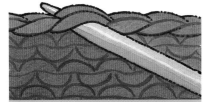

▲ Put your needle through the 12th loop from the center back point.

1 Count 12 cast-on loops from the center back point. Hold the knitting with the reverse stockinette side facing toward you. Put the tip of one of your size 6 (4mm) needles through the 12th loop.

▲ Wrap the yarn around the needle and then knit it in the usual way.

2 Use your finger to wrap the yarn around the needle and then knit it in the usual way.

3 Continue to knit into cast-on loops, working away from the center back until you have 23 stitches on your needle.

4 Now pick up your other needle and begin to work the 23 stitches as seed stitch. (Remember this? It means you need to knit one stitch, purl one stitch right to the end of the row.) Repeat this until you have six rows.

5 Change the color of your yarn and repeat Step 4 until you have 12 rows of seed stitch.

6 Row 13: Purl two stitches together, then knit one, purl one all along the row until you reach the last two stitches. Purl these together.

7 Row 14: Knit two stitches together, then knit one, purl one all along the row until you reach the last two stitches. Knit these together.

8 Repeat Rows 13 and 14 until you have five stitches left (you'll be on Row 21). Then bind off and you've finished one ear.

Left-hand flap

You know how to do this now. Count 34 cast-on loops from the center back point and put the tip of your needle through the 34th loop. Knit into cast-on loops, working toward the center back until you have 23 stitches on your needle. Work in seed stitch as you did for the right-hand flap.

Finishing

Weave in and trim the ends inside the hat. There, you've finished!

Blanket stitch trim

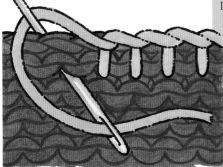

▲ Trim the edge of the hat with blanket stitch.

In a contrasting color yarn, blanket stitch all around the edge of the hat. This is a simple stitch that works well as an edging.

1 Thread a tapestry needle with a long strand of yarn.

2 Start by weaving in the end of the yarn about ½ inch (1cm) from the edge on the wrong side of your knitting.

3 Bring the threaded needle up around the edge of the knitting and stitch through from front to back about two rows in from the edge.

4 The next time you bring the needle up around the edge of the knitting, bring it through the loop of thread that you have just made.

5 Repeat from Step 3. This forms the blanket stitch.

Super circles!

Pompoms

Make three multicolored pompoms
following the instructions on page 16.
Make them as big as you like, but don't
trim the tied ends yet.

Earflap pompoms

▲ Thread three strands of yarn
  through the bottom of the earflap.

1 Using a tapestry needle, thread
three 8-inch (20cm) lengths of yarn
halfway through the bottom point of
an earflap.

▲ Braid the strands together and
  knot the end.

2 Braid the strands together for
about 1½ inches (4cm) and then
tie in a knot to secure.

3 Tie the ends of the braid securely
to the ties on the pompom and
trim the long ends.

4 Repeat Steps 1–3 for the other
earflap pompom.

Top pompom

Using a tapestry needle, stitch the ties
of the final pompom securely through
the point at the top of the hat so that
the pompom sits tightly on the hat. You
did it! Your hat is now ready to wear!

Quick-knit mohair sweater

Knitting your first sweater will take less time than you think. Alternating odd-sized needles, one enormous and one chunky, means that the knitting grows like magic. Here, we stripe the mohair with another bulky yarn to make a lightweight yet cozy knit.

Remember to look at the pictures and instructions on pages 24–31, 54–57, and 70–71 whenever you need help with any of the techniques.

Sizes

Knitting patterns for clothing always include instructions for making different sizes. You could measure one of your favorite sweaters as a guide to which size will be right for you. It is better to make a sweater that is slightly too big than one that is too small. The instructions for the small size are given first, before the parentheses. Inside the parentheses, the first figure refers to the medium size. The second figure in the parentheses is for the large size. To make following the pattern easier, you could circle all the instructions for your size with a pencil before you start knitting. The finished sizes for this sweater are as follows:

Small (medium, large)
Chest at underarm 35 (38, 41) inches or 88 (96, 104) cm
Length from shoulder 20 (22½, 25) inches or 50 (56, 62) cm
Sleeve length 14 (15, 16) inches or 35 (38, 41) cm

Back

Rib hem

1 Using size 11 (8mm) knitting needles and the bulky yarn, cast on 46 (50, 54) stitches.

2 You need to work eight rows in double rib (you practiced this in the Silly Sausages project on page 74).

Row 1: Knit two stitches. *Purl two stitches, knit two stitches.* Repeat the instructions between the asterisks to the end of the row.

Row 2: Purl two stitches. *Knit two stitches, purl two stitches.* Repeat the instructions between the asterisks to the end of the row.

Rows 3–8: Repeat Rows 1 and 2 three more times.

Mohair stripe

1 Swap the empty size 11 (8mm) needle for a big size 19 (15mm) needle. Using the mohair yarn, and with the big needle in your right hand, knit one row. Look at Knitting the Bracelet on pages 36 of the Rainbow Friendship Bands to remind yourself how to tie in a new yarn.

2 With the size 11 (8mm) needle in your right hand, knit one row.

3 With the size 19 (15mm) needle in your right hand, knit one row.

4 With the size 11 (8mm) needle in your right hand, knit one row.

Bulky yarn stripe

1 Swap the empty size 19 (15mm) needle for a size 11 (8mm) needle. Now, going back to using the bulky yarn and size 11 (8mm) needles in both hands, knit one row.

2 Purl one row. Knit one row. Purl one row.

Gauge

Cast on 15 stitches using size 11 (8mm) needles and knit a test piece, following the instructions for Mohair Stripe and Bulky Yarn Stripe. Work two stripes of each color, then measure the gauge (look back at page 92 if you've forgotten how). The gauge for this sweater should be 10 stitches to 4 inches (10cm) and 16 rows to 4¾ inches (12cm). Count the stitches across a bulky yarn stripe. Count the rows down the whole test piece. If you have too many or too few stitches in your test piece, change the size 11 (8mm) needles to a smaller or bigger size and knit another test piece. Keep the size 19 (15mm) needle you use for the bulky yarn stripe the same for the moment. Keep changing the size 11 (8mm) needles and knitting new test pieces until you get the right number of stitches. If you have too few rows at this stage, try changing the size 19 (15mm) needle to a smaller one (you won't have the problem of too many rows).

Continuing the back

1 Repeat the stripe pattern in exactly the same way until you have 8 (9, 10) mohair stripes and 7 (8, 9) bulky yarn stripes.

2 Bind off all the stitches, using two size 11 (8mm) needles. Be careful not to bind off the stitches too tightly.

Front

Make the front of the sweater in exactly the same way as the back until you have 7 (8, 9) mohair stripes and 6 (7, 8) bulky yarn stripes. Do not bind off because you have to shape the neck first.

Shaping the left side of the neck

1 When we refer to the left side of the neck, we mean the side that will be on the left when you're wearing the sweater. Change to the bulky yarn and both size 11 (8mm) needles. Knit the first 16 (17, 19) stitches of the row.

2 Knit the next two stitches in the row together.

3 Slip the rest of the stitches onto a stitch holder. Look back at page 85 of Floppy Dollies to remind yourself how to do this. You can ignore these stitches until later. You now have 17 (18, 20) stitches left on the needle. Turn the work.

4 Purl the first two stitches together, then purl to the end of the row. You now have 16 (17, 19) stitches on the needle.

5 Knit the first 14 (15, 17) stitches, then knit the last two stitches together. You have 15 (16, 18) stitches on the needle.

6 Purl the first two stitches together, then purl to the end of the row. You have 14 (15, 17) stitches on the needle.

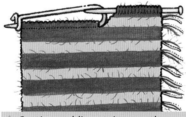

▲ Continue adding stripes on the left side of the neck.

7 Change to the mohair yarn, and with the size 19 (15mm) needle in your right hand, knit one row.

8 With the size 11 (8mm) needle in your right hand, knit one row.

9 With the size 19 (15mm) needle in your right hand, knit one row.

10 With the size 11 (8mm) needle in your right hand, knit one row.

11 Bind off all 14 (15, 17) stitches using the size 11 (8mm) needles.

Materials

● 240 (275, 310) yards or 220 (250, 280) meters of bulky yarn

● 135 (165, 200) yards or 120 (150, 180) meters of mohair yarn

● Size 11 (8mm) knitting needles

● One size 19 (15mm) knitting needle

● Size 10½ (7mm) knitting needles

● Stitch holder

● Scissors

● Tapestry needle

● 2 large towels

● Pins

● Tape measure

● Safety pins

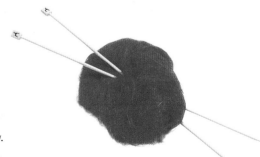

Shaping the right side of the neck

1 When we refer to the right side of the neck, we mean the side that will be on the right when you're wearing the sweater. Slip the first 18 (19, 21) stitches onto a size 11 (8mm) needle. Leave the remaining 10 (12, 12) stitches on the stitch holder. These stitches are at the center front of the neck.

2 Rejoin the yarn. Using both size 11 (8mm) needles and the bulky yarn, knit the first two stitches together, then knit the remaining 16 (17, 19) stitches.

3 Purl the first 15 (16, 18) stitches, then purl the last two stitches together. You have 16 (17, 19) stitches on the needle.

4 Knit the first two stitches together, then knit to the end of the row. You have 15 (16, 18) stitches on the needle.

5 Purl the first 13 (14, 16) stitches, then purl the last two stitches together. You now have 14 (15, 17) stitches on the needle.

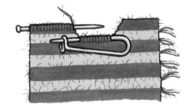

▲ Continue adding stripes on the right side of the neck.

6 Change to the mohair yarn, and with the size 19 (15mm) needle in your right hand, knit one row.

7 With the size 11 (8mm) needle in your right hand, knit one row.

8 With the size 19 (15mm) needle in your right hand, knit one row.

9 With the size 11 (8mm) needle in your right hand, knit one row.

10 Bind off all 14 (15, 17) stitches using the size 11 (8mm) needles.

Sleeves

You need to knit two sleeves in exactly the same way.

Rib cuff

1 Using the size 11 (8mm) needles and the bulky yarn, cast on 22 (26, 26) stitches.

2 You need to work eight rows in double rib.

Row 1: Knit two stitches. *Purl two stitches, knit two stitches.* Repeat the instructions between the asterisks to the end of the row.

Row 2: Purl two stitches. *Knit two stitches, purl two stitches.* Repeat the instructions between the asterisks to the end of the row.

3 Repeat these Rows 1 and 2 three more times.

More mohair stripes

1 You are now going to knit four rows in mohair yarn, just like you did for the back and front of the sweater. Swap the empty size 11 (8mm) needle for the size 19 (15mm) needle. Using the mohair yarn, and holding the big needle in your right hand, knit one row.

2 With the size 11 (8mm) needle in your right hand, knit one row.

3 With the size 19 (15mm) needle in your right hand, knit one row.

4 With the size 11 (8mm) needle in your right hand, knit one row.

Bulky yarn stripe with increasing

The sleeves need to be shaped so that they become wider as you work up the arm. Swap the empty size 19 (15mm) needle for a size 11 (8mm) needle and change to the bulky yarn.

1 Knit one row, increasing at both ends of the row by knitting twice into the first stitch and then knitting twice into the last stitch (this is the bar increase method that you learned on page 55). You now have 24 (28, 28) stitches.

2 Purl all of the stitches on the next row of the sleeve.

3 Knit one row, increasing at both ends like you did in Step 1. You now have 26 (30, 30) stitches.

4 Purl all of the stitches on the next row of the sleeve.

Finishing the sleeve

1 Repeat the mohair and bulky yarn stripes, always increasing on the knit rows of the bulky yarn stripe, until you have 5 (5, 6) mohair stripes and 4 (4, 5) bulky yarn stripes. You should have 38 (42, 46) stitches on your needle.

2 Change to the bulky yarn and work 1 (2, 1) stripes without increasing any stitches. You should now have 10 (11, 12) stripes in total. The last stripe will be different for different sizes to get the correct sleeve length. The last stripe for the small size will be a bulky yarn stripe. The last stripe for the medium size will be a mohair stripe. The last stripe for the large size will be a bulky yarn stripe.

3 Bind off all the stitches. Now knit the second sleeve in the same way.

Warm and cuddly!

Project 14

Assembling the sweater

Blocking

1 You need to make sure that all the pieces of your sweater are the right size before joining the seams. First, you will need to block the pieces just like you did with the Plaid Poncho on page 95. Do not pin out the ribs when blocking; let them relax into shape.

2 The back and front should be the same size: 17½ (19, 20½) inches or 44 (48, 52) cm wide and 20 (22½, 25) inches or 50 (56, 62) cm long. Both sleeves should be 14 (15, 16) inches or 35 (38, 41) cm long.

Right shoulder seam

1 Pin the front and back pieces together at the right shoulder seam, right sides facing.

2 Use mohair yarn and a small overcast stitch to sew up the seam, like you did for the Funny-face Bag on page 34.

Neckband

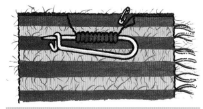

▲ Mark the the position of the neck on the back piece of the sweater.

1 Lay the front piece of the sweater on top of the back piece. Use a stitch marker or safety pin to mark the place where the left side of the neck opening will be on the back piece. Don't pin the two pieces together.

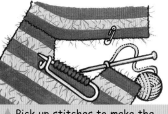

▲ Pick up stitches to make the neckband.

2 Start making the neckband at the left shoulder on the front piece of knitting, with the right side of the knitting facing you. Use the bulky yarn and a size 10½ (7mm) knitting needle to pick up and knit twice into the first stitch. Look at Making the Neckband for the Plaid Poncho on page 96 to remind you how to do this. Pick up and knit nine more stitches down the left side of the neck.

3 Knit across the 10 (12, 12) stitches on the stitch holder at the center front.

4 Pick up and knit ten stitches up the right front neck shaping.

5 Pick up and knit 17 (19, 19) stitches across the back piece of the sweater as far as the safety pin. Knit twice into the last stitch. You now have 50 (54, 54) stitches on the needle.

6 Pick up your second size 10½ (7mm) needle. Work four rows in double rib, starting with purl two stitches.

7 Bind off loosely. You have now finished the neckband.

Sewing the seams

1 Sew the left shoulder seam in the same way as you sewed the right.

2 Weave in all the loose ends to neaten the pieces before continuing.

Sewing sleeves in

1 Lay the sweater out, right side facing you, so that the shoulder seams are spread open. Fold a sleeve in half lengthwise to find the center and measure the width at the top.

▲ Mark the position of the sleeves on the body of the sweater.

2 Measure this distance from the shoulder seam down the front and then down the back of the sweater. Use a safety pin or knot of yarn to mark this point at the edge of the fabric.

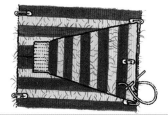

▲ Sew the first sleeve in place.

3 With right sides together, lay the first sleeve in place, on the body, between the markers. Match the center of the sleeve to the shoulder seam and pin in place.

4 Use a small overcast stitch to join the seam. Repeat for the second sleeve on the other side of the sweater.

Mattress stitch

For the rest of the seams, you are going to use mattress stitch. This is really useful because it creates a seam that is invisible from the right side. It will also give you a really accurate way of matching the stripes.

1 Lay the pieces to be joined flat and edge to edge. The right side of the knitting should face upward.

2 Thread a tapestry needle with the bulky yarn and attach the yarn with a small stitch to the back of one piece of knitting.

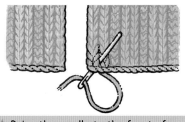

▲ Bring the needle to the front of the knitting between the first two stitches.

3 Sew through from the back to the front, bringing the needle out between the edge stitch and the second stitch in the first row.

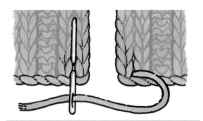

▲ Cross the needle over to the second piece of knitting.

4 Insert the needle between the edge stitch and the second stitch in the first row on the other piece of knitting. Pass the needle under the loop to the row above, then bring it back through to the front.

▲ Now bring the needle back to the first piece of knitting.

5 Insert the needle into the hole that the stitch on the first side came out of. Pass it under the loop to the row above, even with the opposite side.

6 Repeat this process to make a zigzag between the edges. Make sure that you keep the sides even and do not miss any rows.

▲ Pull the yarn gently to close up the seam after about five or six rows.

7 After about five or six rows, gently pull the yarn to close the seam, then continue sewing mattress stitch to the end of the seam.

8 Use mattress stitch to sew up the side seams, sleeves, and the rib at the neck. Take your time so that you get a really neat result.

Warm and cuddly!

Project 14

You have now made your first sweater. With all the techniques that you have learned, there's no reason why you shouldn't try other clothing patterns.

Help! I have no yarn

Don't worry. Whether you've knitted with every leftover piece of yarn that you can find, or you want to try knitting with something different, you can make alternative "yarns" by recycling outgrown clothes or plastic grocery bags. You can even knit with string and videotape. These "yarns" are perfect for making unique rag rugs and rag bags.

Making your own yarn

Making your own yarn is really easy, and by using it you will be able to knit things that are completely unique. Once you start looking around, you will realize that you have all that you need to make your first ball of yarn. Here are some ideas to get you started, but you will soon be coming up with your own.

Rag yarn

All you need to make yarn is a pair of scissors or pinking shears and lots of unwanted fabric. The easiest weight of fabric to start with is that of worn-out or outgrown clothes, such as shirts or T-shirts. You could also try old sheets, pillowcases, duvets, drapes, tablecloths, or fabric remnants from a sewing store.

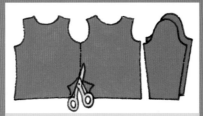

▲ Cut any clothing along the seams and lay the pieces flat.

1 First of all, cut any clothing apart along the seams so that the pieces lie more or less flat.

▲ Look closely at woven fabric to see where the straight grain is.

2 Look closely at the fabric. Woven fabrics, such as linen and cotton,

are made up of straight lines of threads that have been woven together. Half the lines will go up and down, and the other half weave in and out of them from side to side. These straight lines are called the "straight grain" of the fabric.

▲ Cut or tear woven fabric into strips.

3 Cut or tear a straight line along the edge of the woven fabric, following the straight grain. Most woven fabrics will tear straight along the grain if you make a small snip at the edge of the fabric first.

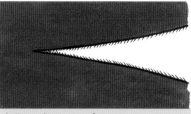

▲ Tear the strips if you want a frayed edge.

▲ Pull the strips gently to be sure they are strong enough.

4 If you tear the strips, the yarn you are making will have a nice frayed edge.

▲ Use pinking shears to cut strips with a zigzag edge.

5 Try cutting the fabric with pinking shears if you want to make yarn with a zigzag edge.

6 It is usually better to cut rather than tear jersey fabrics, like T-shirts. These will make yarn with a rolled edge.

▲ Cut up jersey fabric with scissors to make yarn with a rolled edge.

7 Decide how wide you want the yarn to be. A strip that is about ¼–¾ inch (1–2cm) wide is suitable for most fabrics. Do not cut heavier fabrics, like denim, too wide or the yarn will be too bulky to knit. Gently pull both ends of the first strip you cut to make sure it does not fall apart. If it is too weak, try cutting a little wider for the rest of the strips.

8 Now simply cut or tear lots of strips in the same way.

▲ Tie the strips together and roll them up into a ball.

9 To make your strips into yarn, tie the ends together to make a long length. You could mix lots of different colors together and make one huge, multicolored ball of yarn, or divide them into several balls of separate colors for knitting stripes. As you tie the strips together, roll the yarn you are making into a ball so that it doesn't get tangled.

Rag yarn is ideal for making rugs and bags (see pages 114–119), or even for making funny-looking juggling balls. Always check with an adult before you start cutting things up, though!

Plastic bag yarn

This yarn is great for making a waterproof mat or a useful swim bag. This time you just need your scissors and lots of plastic bags.

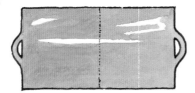

▲ Cut each bag open and lay it flat.

1 Cut the sides of the bags open so that they lie flat. Cut off any handles.

2 Cut a straight line along the edge of the bag, then fold ¾–1½ inches (2–4cm) of the plastic over the blade of the scissors at the edge you have just cut. It is best to fold over a narrow strip of plastic if you are using thick bags, or a wider strip if you are using thin, lightweight bags.

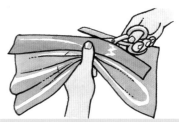

▲ Slide a pair of scissors along the fold to cut a strip of plastic.

3 Pinch the folded bag firmly between the fingers of one hand, then use your other hand to slide the scissors along the fold, cutting the plastic. This is a quick way to slice the plastic into strips. Keep the bag taut as you cut.

4 Tie the plastic strips together to make balls of yarn, like you did for the rag yarn.

Other types of yarn

When you think about it, you will soon realize that you can knit with any long, flexible strip or thread. Here are some more yarn ideas that you may like to try for fun. Just ask permission before you start knitting.

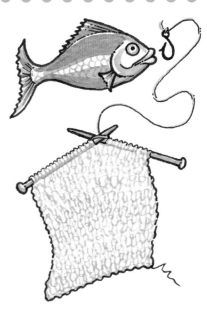

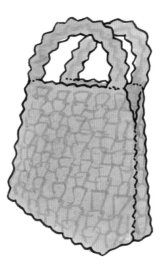

● **String** or **garden twine** is a cheap alternative to conventional yarn and is already in a ball. It knits into a strong, open fabric.

● **Raffia** is good for knitting a natural-style beach bag or mat.

● **Fishing line** is great for creating invisible knitting, so try putting an invisible stripe into your work.

Let it rip!

Recycling yarn

A traditional method of reusing yarn is to unravel unwanted knitted garments. Use a small pair of scissors to pick seams apart and cut the bind-off stitches at the top of the knitting. The fabric will unravel surprisingly quickly. Ball up each length of yarn as you go. This recycled yarn is great for knitting small toys and dolls' clothes, or knit lots of squares to make a patchwork blanket.

Different fabrics will make different types of yarn. You can even make a really springy, lightweight yarn from stockings and panty hose that have runs!

● **Fine-gauge wire** knits into a wonderful, flexible fabric that you can mold into different shapes. Try making mini sculptures or a spectacular metal version of one of the Fantastic Flowers on pages 42–47. You will need to fold in the ends of the wire carefully so that they don't catch on your clothes or other fabrics.

● **Videotape, clothesline, shoelaces** ... the list is almost endless.

● **Ribbons** and **braid** can be used to make an attractive trim for other pieces of knitting. Just knit a few rows with it, then stitch it in place.

Now you will never run out of yarn. Just be inventive and you can always keep knitting.

Rag rug and bag

A new lease on life for old shirts and dresses, this rug is suitable for the bathroom or bedroom, or as a sleeping mat for a favorite pet. Try the same thing with recycled plastic bags and you will have a waterproof picnic blanket. You could even fold a rag-knitted rectangle in half and add handles to make a strong, unique bag that will last forever.

These projects are really easy. To make the yarn, look back at the instructions on pages 110–113, then use the basic knitting skills you learned on pages 24–31.

Rag rug

It is difficult to specify the quantity of yarn needed for this project, because every rag yarn is a bit different. However, as a guide, our rag rug used about 1¼ pounds (600g) of light- to medium-weight cotton fabrics that had been cut into strips ¾ inch (2cm) wide. You could weigh your yarn on a kitchen scale to check that you have enough, but it's easy to make more if you need to.

Save some of the cast-on yarn to use at the bottom edge of the rug before you bind off, so that both ends behave in the same way.

Materials

- About 14 ounces (400g) of rag yarn in the main color

- About 7 ounces (200g) of rag yarn in the second color

- Several small balls of rag yarn in contrasting colors

- Size 19 (15mm) knitting needles

- Scissors

Knotty knitting!

Starting the rug

1 Cast on 30–40 stitches in the main color. Cast on in the usual way, keeping the stitches quite loose, so that you will be able to knit into them easily. If they are too close together on the needle, you will find knitting difficult.

2 Now, working in knit stitch, complete the first row. Knit loosely, so that the stitches can slide along the needles easily. When you come to a knot in the yarn, just keep knitting

and the ends of the knot will become part of the fabric design.

3 At the end of the row, simply turn the knitting and continue in knit stitch as you would when knitting with ordinary yarn. You need to knit a total of six rows of the main color, and then you can start adding stripes.

Knitting stripes

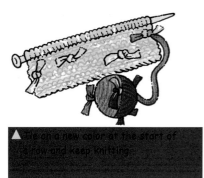

▲ Tie on a new color at the start of a row and keep knitting.

1 To change color at the end of a row, cut the yarn, leaving a short tail. Tie on the second color so that the knot sits by the needle, and start knitting the next row in the new yarn.

2 Knit the next two rows in the second color.

3 Repeat Steps 1–2 to add lots more colorful stripes to your rug. It will look good if you knit a stripe for just a single row now and then (in other words, just do Step 1).

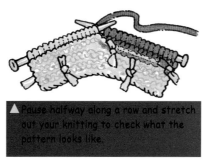

▲ Pause halfway along a row and stretch out your knitting to check what the pattern looks like.

4 As you knit, you will start to get a good idea of how far your yarn goes. This will make it easier to plan your stripe pattern. If you pause halfway across a row, you can stretch out the width of the rug more easily and look at the stripes.

5 When your rug is almost as long as you wish, change back to the main color and knit a few rows. When you are happy with the length and look of your rug, you need to bind off. Do this in the usual way, but be very careful not to bind off tightly, because this will gather in one end of the rug so that it is narrower than the rest.

Finishing the rug

Lay the rug out flat and trim any ends that you think are too long. The random knots are part of the design of a rag rug. If you want even more knots, you can cut some short lengths of rag yarn and tie them into the knitting wherever you like.

Next you could try knitting a plastic bag rug to use as a mat for sitting on outdoors. Use smaller needles—size 15 (10mm) would be good.

Rag bag

This bag has been knitted with multicolored rag yarn, made by knotting together random strips of different light- to medium-weight fabrics. The strips were cut about ½ inch (1.5cm) wide.

Materials

● About 7 ounces (200g) of multicolored rag yarn

- - - - - - - - - - - - - - -

● Ball of string

- - - - - - - - - - - - - - -

● Size 15 (10mm) knitting needles

- - - - - - - - - - - - - - -

● Scissors

- - - - - - - - - - - - - - -

● Large tapestry needle

Starting the bag

1 Cast on 30 stitches using the multicolored rag yarn.

2 Work the first four rows in knit stitch.

3 Cut the yarn, leaving a short tail. Tightly tie on the end of a ball of string, with the knot close to the needle. Knit six rows in string.

4 Cut the string, leaving a short tail, and tie on the rag yarn once again. Knit four rows in rag yarn.

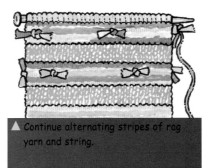

▲ Continue alternating stripes of rag yarn and string.

5 Continue striping the string and rag yarn until the knitting is twice as long as you want your finished bag to be. Finish with four rows of rag yarn and bind off.

Sewing up the bag

1 Fold the knitting in half to make the bag shape. Make sure the cast-on and bind-off edges meet at the top.

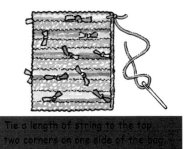

▲ Tie a length of string to the top two corners on one side of the bag.

2 Cut a 24-inch (60cm) length of string and tie the end securely through the cast-on and bind-off stitches at the top of the bag, on one side. Thread the string onto a large tapestry needle.

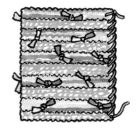

▲ Overcast the seams securely.

3 Use an overcast stitch to join the seam securely, sewing into each stitch at the edge of the bag, like you did on page 34 of the Funny-face Bag. Sew a few stitches one on top of the other to secure the end.

4 Weave the end of the string into the knitting and tie to the nearest knot in the yarn.

5 Repeat Steps 2–4 on the other side of the bag.

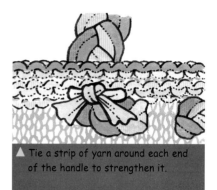

Making handles

1 Cut six lengths of rag yarn about 20 inches (50cm) long each.

2 Tie them all together at one end, leaving tails 2 inches (5cm) long.

▲ Braid the yarn and knot the ends securely.

3 Divide the lengths of yarn into three bunches (there'll be two pieces of yarn in each bunch). Braid the bunches of yarn for 14 inches (35cm). If you need a reminder, we did braiding on page 17. Knot the end of the braid to secure it.

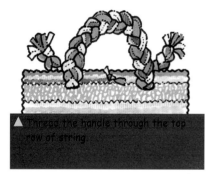

▲ Thread the handle through the top row of string.

4 Thread both ends of the braid through the top edge of one side of the bag to make a handle. Thread it through the top row of string from the outside of the bag to the inside. The handle should be in the center of the edge, and the ends should be threaded through about 4 inches (10cm) apart.

▲ Weave the ends of the braid into the middle and knot them together.

5 Weave each end in and out of the stitches, working toward the center of the bag, and tie them together on the wrong side of the fabric so that the ends of the braid join to form a strong handle. Trim the ends of the braid.

▲ Tie a strip of yarn around each end of the handle to strengthen it.

6 Tie a 4-inch (10cm) length of rag yarn through the top row of knitting and around the handle on each side, to hold it in place. Trim the ends.

7 Repeat Steps 1–6 to make a second handle, and your bag is ready to go.

Lining the bag

The bag is great for carrying things like groceries, schoolbooks, a football, or balls of yarn, but if you want to carry smaller items, like knitting needles or pencils, you will need to sew lining inside to keep things from falling out.

Materials

● Piece of fabric to fit inside bag (see Step 1 below)

- - - - - - - - - - - - - - - - - -

● Pins

- - - - - - - - - - - - - - - - - -

● Sewing thread and needle

- - - - - - - - - - - - - - - - - -

● Scissors

▲ Figure out the size of fabric you will need to fit inside the bag.

1 Measure the width of your bag and add 1 inch (3cm); write this number down. Measure the length of your bag, multiply it by 2, then add 1½ inches (4cm); write this number down. Lay out the piece of fabric and measure the width and length you have written down. Cut out the fabric to this size.

2 Fold the fabric in half, right sides together, and pin the edges.

3 Thread the sewing needle and knot both ends together to double the thread. Backstitch the seam, like we did on page 76 of the Silly Sausages project, ½ inch (1.5cm) in from the edge. Keep the stitches quite small and neat. This will make a strong seam.

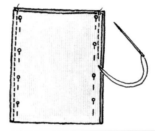

▲ Backstitch both seams.

4 Repeat Step 3 for the other seam, then remove the pins.

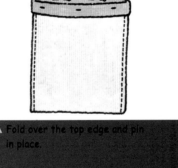
▲ Fold over the top edge and pin in place.

5 Fold the top edge over ¾ inch (2cm) to the wrong side. Pin from the right side to hold the fold in place.

6 Place the lining inside the bag so that the folded top edge is ¾ inch (2cm) below the top of the bag. Use a few more pins to hold the fabric in place.

▲ Overcast the top of the lining to the bag.

7 Overcast the lining into the bag, stitching over the edge of the fold and into the rag yarn all the way around the top of the lining.

8 Remove the pins and your lining is complete.

Rag yarn is ideal for making unique knitted items. Why not try making a smaller version of the bag with longer straps to use as a shoulder bag?

Now all you have to do is decide what to keep in your new bag. The instructions will produce a bag that is just the right size to store your knitting equipment and knitting projects.

Oh, no! What went wrong?

When learning any new skill, you are bound to find that some things don't turn out as planned. The first thing to remember is DON'T PANIC. Even the most experienced knitters occasionally make a mistake. With time and practice you will learn that it is always easier to correct any problems as soon as you spot them.

Getting help

A problem often seems much smaller if somebody can help you with it. If you need guidance, ask another knitter for advice. If somebody in your household can knit, that person may be able to help. Find out if any of your teachers knit. You will probably find lots of willing advice at your local yarn or craft store. If you can't find anybody to help you, look at this list of common problems and you may find a solution. Also reread the instructions in the projects to make sure that you are following them correctly.

Oh, no! My knitting looks uneven

Tension the yarn

It takes practice to get the tension of the yarn even. Review Holding the Yarn on page 27 and remind yourself how to tension the yarn with your fingers. You may find that you can add tension by holding the working end of the yarn between your knees or running it over your shoulder.

Reposition your stitches

While you are knitting, try to keep the stitches toward the tips of the needles so that they don't get too stretched.

Finish the row

Finish a row before stopping your knitting, because stitches get stretched and may even get dropped if you stop halfway.

Wash it

Washing a garment or piece of knitting will often help to even up the stitches. Follow the instructions on the ball band and in Caring for Your Knitting on page 125 to see how to do this.

Oh, no! My knitting is the wrong size

Check the gauge

If your knitting is the wrong size, the first thing to do is to check the gauge. Refer to page 92 to review the information about gauge. Always make a test piece before starting a garment, or it may not fit.

Keep count

You may have cast on too many or too few stitches, or knitted the wrong number of rows, so check the pattern. It is a good idea to use a pencil and paper to count the rows as you knit them, and also to check, now and again, that you have the right number of stitches in a row. If you are using a pattern that has different sizes, make sure that you have circled all the instructions for the size you are knitting.

Oh, no! There are too many stitches in the row

Check the position of your yarn

Your yarn may be in the wrong place at the beginning or in the middle of a row. When you are about to do a knit stitch, the yarn should be behind the needle before you make the stitch. When you are about to do a purl stitch, the yarn should be in front of the needle before you make the stitch. If the yarn is in the wrong place, you will create an extra loop that will look like a stitch—this is like accidentally making a yarnover. You will be able to see a little hole in the row where you made the mistake.

Check your stitch technique

You may have knitted twice into a stitch, like increasing. Make sure you always slip the stitch off the left needle before working into the next stitch. Make sure you are knitting only into the stitch on the left needle and not knitting into the strand between two stitches.

Pick up the whole stitch

You may have split a stitch into two and worked into it twice. This can happen with loosely twisted or very textured yarns, or when you are knitting two ends of yarn together. Be very careful to pick up the whole stitch and not to push the needle through the middle of the yarn.

Oh, no! There aren't enough stitches in the row

Knit one stitch at a time

You may have accidentally knitted two stitches together, like decreasing. Make sure that you knit into only one stitch at a time. Use your fingertip to spread apart the stitches at the tip of the left needle if they are sitting very close together.

Look for a dropped stitch

You may have dropped a stitch, so refer to Oh, No! I've Dropped a Stitch (see right).

Oh, no! I've dropped a stitch

Pick it up again

Slightly different techniques are used to pick up stitches, depending on what stitch pattern you knit. You learned how to pick up a dropped garter stitch on page 49 of the Supersize Scarf. The methods of picking up both knit and purl stockinette stitches are explained in the Dressy Clutch Bag on page 80. You can see how to mend a stockinette stitch ladder in the Plaid Poncho on pages 94–95. If you get a ladder when you are working in garter stitch, count the number of strands in the ladder. If there is an even number, start at Step 1 below. If there is an odd number, start at Step 3.

Even number of strands

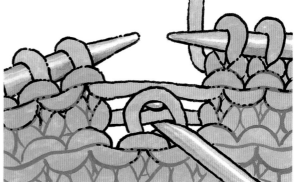

1 Push a crochet hook through the loop at the bottom of the ladder, from front to back, and then catch the strand above the loop in the hook.

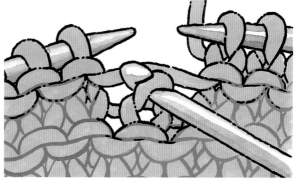

2 Pull the strand through the stitch on the hook. The strand has now become a new stitch. Carefully remove the hook from the stitch. If you now have an odd number of strands, continue with Step 3. If you have reached the top of the ladder, go to Step 5.

Odd number of strands

3 Push a crochet hook through the loop at the bottom of the ladder, from back to front, and then catch the strand above the loop in the hook.

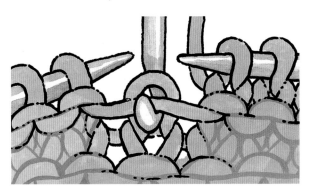

4 Pull the strand through the stitch on the hook to make a new stitch. You will now have an even number of strands in the ladder (unless you have reached the top). Carefully remove the hook from the stitch.

5 Alternate the instructions for even and odd numbers of strands until all the strands have been made into stitches. Lift the last stitch onto the left needle, making sure that it doesn't get twisted, and continue to work the row.

Oh, no! My cast on and bind off are too tight . . . or too loose

Undo the knitting

Examine the cast-on after you have knitted a few rows. If it looks wrong, undo the knitting and start again because you will not be able to correct this when the knitting is finished. The cast-on row needs to be a bit stretchy, like the knitting. If it is too tight, it will pull the knitting in. Check the bind-off after the first few stitches so that you do not have to unravel the whole row and do it again.

Use bigger or smaller needles

If your cast-on is too tight, try using a needle one size bigger than the knitting for the first row, then change to the recommended size needle for the rest of the pattern. If the cast-on is too loose, try using a needle one size smaller for the cast-on row. This is important if you are knitting a springy rib to pull in at the edge of a sweater. Lots of patterns recommend using smaller sized needles for all the rib trims on a garment. If the bind-off is too tight, you can try changing to a needle one size bigger for the bind-off row. You may have problems getting a sweater over your head if the bind-off is too tight. If the bind-off is too loose and pulls the knitting out, try using a smaller needle for the bind-off row to make it tighter.

Oh, no! My yarn is running out

Start a new ball

Each row of knitting uses a piece of yarn about three times the width of the knitting. If you do not have a length of yarn that measures about four times the width of the knitting, change to a new ball so that you will have plenty of yarn to complete the row.

Buy an extra ball

It is always better to buy an extra ball of yarn before you start making something even though most patterns build in an extra amount. You can always use spare yarn on a smaller project. Most stores will gladly give a refund or store credit for unused balls of yarn if you provide a receipt. However, it's always best to ask about store policy before you buy.

Buy matching yarn

If you do need to buy more yarn after you've started a project, you will need to match the shade number and dye lot of your original yarn. Look at the ball band of the previous ball and check the details, as listed in Ball Band Information on page 9. Go back to the store where you bought the yarn and see if it has any in stock—you may be lucky. It is not a good idea to change to a different dye lot in the middle of a single-color piece of knitting because it will show up as a stripe. If you really have no choice, try knitting the new color where it will be less obvious; for example, on the trim or for a whole section.

Oh, no! I can't find the right yarn

Check the ball band

Most patterns suggest a suitable weight of yarn to use. If the pattern has to be a certain size, like a sweater, it is important to find a yarn that knits to the correct gauge— look at Ball Band Information on page 9 and Measuring Gauge on page 92. Sometimes it won't matter if the knitting comes out a bit smaller or bigger; for example, a bag or a scarf. In this case, look at the ball bands on a number of yarns to find one that has a similar weight and see which needles are recommended.

Oh, no! I need to unravel some of my knitting

Ask for help or start again

Unraveling rows of knitting is quite difficult for a beginner, so if somebody offers to help you, always say "Yes, please" with a big smile. If you have knitted only a few rows when you spot a mistake, it may be quicker and easier to start the whole piece again.

Unravel stitch by stitch

If the mistake is on the same row on which you are currently working, unravel your knitting stitch by stitch to right before the mistake.

1 On a knit row, insert the tip of the left-hand needle, from front to back, into the stitch immediately below the first stitch on the right-hand needle. Slip the stitch onto the left needle.

2 Gently pull the working end of the yarn to undo the stitch above the one you slipped onto the left needle. Continue in this way until you have reached the stitch before you made the mistake.

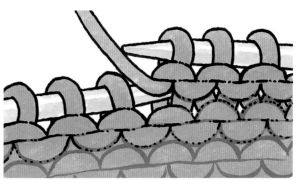

3 On a purl row, insert the tip of the left-hand needle, from front to back, into the stitch immediately below the first stitch on the right-hand needle. Slip the stitch onto the left needle.

4 Gently pull the working end of the yarn to undo the stitch above the one you slipped onto the left needle. Continue in this way until you have reached the stitch before you made the mistake.

123

Unravel row by row

If the mistake is on a previous row, unravel your knitting row by row back to before you made the mistake. Be patient and don't try to rush. If you have been making a note of the number of rows you have knitted as part of your pattern, don't forget to count how many rows you unravel so that you know where you are in the pattern after you have finished unraveling.

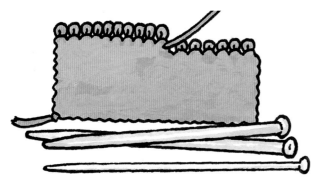

1 Find a knitting needle that is thinner than the one you were knitting with.

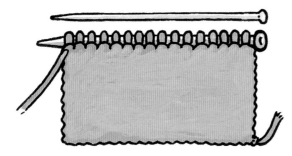

2 Lay the knitting on a flat, clean surface. Slide the stitches off the needle and pull the yarn gently to unravel the knitting and leave the row with the mistake at the top of the knitting. Do this slowly and very carefully.

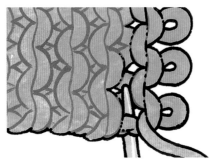

3 Lay the knitting sideways so that the working end of the yarn appears from the bottom right-hand corner. Insert the tip of the thinner needle into the stitch below the first unraveled loop, pointing toward the other end of the row and coming from the back to the front of the stitch.

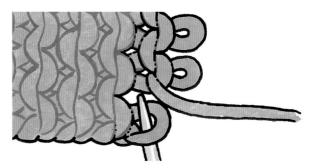

4 Gently pull the end of the yarn to unravel the loop as far as the next stitch.

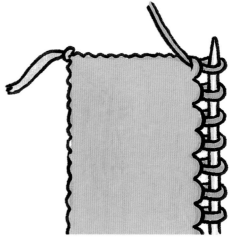

5 Pick up the stitches one at a time along the row in this way, unraveling the wrong row as you go. You will end up with all the stitches on the thinner needle. Breathe a sigh of relief—you have saved your knitting. Well done.

6 Now, using one of the correct size needles, work the next row. Make sure that you continue the pattern from the right place.

7 Put down the thinner needle and continue with the pattern using both correct needles.

Caring for your knitting

You have put a lot of effort into making your own hand-knitted things, so you will want to keep them looking good and make them last a long time.

Washing

Some yarns, especially synthetic fibers, can be machine washed. Other yarns, like wool, need to be washed by hand. Follow the washing instructions on the yarn's ball band. If you lose the band or are not sure how to wash your yarn, always hand wash in lukewarm water.

Hand washing

1 Dissolve some mild detergent recommended for your fibers in lukewarm water. Gently squeeze the knitting in the soapy water to loosen the dirt. Do not rub the fabric. Leave the knitting in the water for about five minutes.

2 Let the water drain away, then gently squeeze out as much water as you can. Add fresh lukewarm water and squeeze the knitting to rinse away the suds. Drain the water and repeat until the water is clear.

3 Gently squeeze out the water and then lay the garment flat on a thick, dry, colorfast towel. Roll up the towel with the knitting inside and press down on the roll to help the towel absorb most of the water.

4 Lay out another dry towel, away from direct sunlight or heat sources like radiators, and put the garment on it. The garment should be laid flat and pulled into its usual shape and size. Leave it like this until completely dry.

Machine washing

Stick to the recommended temperature on the yarn's ball band and use the gentlest setting possible. You can place the garment inside a pillowcase before putting it in the machine to prevent it from stretching. Take the knitted piece out of the machine as soon as the cycle has finished. Dry the garment by following Step 4 of Hand Washing. If you are unsure about the washing instructions, or do not have permission or help to use a machine, hand wash instead.

Storing

Do not put your knitting on a hanger because it will stretch and pull out of shape. Instead, fold knitted items and store them in a drawer or on a shelf. If your knitting is to be stored for a long time, make sure it is clean before you put it away. Moths love to spoil woollen garments by stealing fibers to make their cocoons. You can protect the garments from moths by using a natural moth repellent such as cedar chips. Try to keep stored knits sealed in a plastic bag or shake them out in the daylight regularly.

Washing Symbols

 40°C 104°F — Machine washable at the maximum water temperature shown inside the symbol

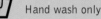 Hand wash only

Hot iron

Warm iron

Cool iron

Can be treated with bleach

Can be tumble dried

Dry cleanable

A large cross through any of the symbols means that you should not use that process on your yarn—for example, a cross through a symbol of an iron means "Do not iron."

Understanding patterns

The projects in this book have been explained clearly in a step-by-step way so that a beginner can easily follow them. If you have ever looked at the instructions in other knitting patterns, you may have noticed that they are written very differently.

Don't be put off

Knitting patterns are usually written without full sentences and use lots of strange words that you probably won't recognize. These odd-looking words are just abbreviations for the same knitting instructions you've been using in this book. Following a pattern is usually quite easy because everything is written in the right order and uses more or less the same terms and abbreviations. Some patterns include an alphabetical list of abbreviations and an explanation of what they all mean, but knitters soon learn the most commonly used ones. If you do see an abbreviation that is not on the list shown here, check the information on the pattern to see if it is explained, or ask a more experienced knitter to help you translate.

Example

With a bit of practice, you will find that reading patterns comes easily to you. Start by looking at this set of instructions and guess what you would have knitted (the answer is on page 128).

the answer is on page 128

Sizes: small (medium, large)
CO 10 sts using size 8 (5mm) needles and worsted-weight cotton yarn.
Row 1. K to end.
Rep this row 5 more times.
*Row 7. (k2tog.) Rep to end of row.
Row 8. K to end.
Rep this row 7 more times.
Row 16. (kfb) rep to end of row.
Row 17. K to end.
Rep this row 5 more times.
Rep from * 4 (5,6) more times.
BO all sts.

Common abbreviations

alt	alternate
beg	beginning
BO	bind off
CC	contrast color
CO	cast on
col	color
cm	centimeters
cont	continue
dec	decrease/decreasing
dpn	double-pointed needles
foll	following
g, gr, or gm	grams
G st	garter stitch
in	inches
inc	increase/increasing
k	knit
kfb	knit into front and back of stitch (increasing)
k2tog	knit 2 together
LH	left hand
lp	loop
meas	measures
m	meters
MC	main color
oz	ounce(s)
p	purl
pat(t)	pattern
psso	pass slip stitch(es) over
rem	remaining
rep	repeat
RH	right hand
rib	ribbing
rnds or rds	rounds
RS	right side
sl	slip
sl st	slip stitch
st(s)	stitch(es)
st st	stockinette stitch
tbl	through back of loop
tog	together
WS	wrong side
wyib	with yarn in back
wyif	with yarn in front
yd(s)	yard(s)
yo	yarn over needle (to make extra stitch)
"	inches
* or ( )	asterisks or parentheses are used to show a set of instructions that need to be repeated a stated number of times

Index

Credits

Quarto would like to thank Ashley Beattie, Ryan Harris, Arabel Jordan, Charlotte Knight, Hettie Reatchlous, Tattie Reatchlous, Alex Sesiuk, Jack Sesiuk, Freya Tomley, and Milly Wright for modeling the projects in this book. All photographs and illustrations are the copyright of Quarto.

Author's acknowledgments
Thanks to my lovely knitting mum Helen Clewer for lots of help and inspiration, and to Tiphaine de Lussy, Rachel Cattle, Alison Cooke, and Zena Barrie for being such enthusiastic knitters and pompom makers!

Answer to knitting pattern example on page 126: You would have knitted the Desert Island Belt project from pages 62–65.